TRANSFORM

TRANSFORM

Tune In to Turn On Your Authentic Self

JONI L. DAVIS

Licensed Marriage and Family Therapist

TRANSFORMATION TOWN
press

Published by Transformation Town Press, Long Beach
jonildavis.com

ISBN (paperback): 979-8-9948532-0-7
ISBN (ebook): 979-8-9948532-1-4
ISBN (audiobook): 979-8-9948532-2-1

First edition

CONTENTS

PART I: GET TO KNOW YOUR INSIDES

PART II: STEPS TO TRANSFORMING UNMET NEEDS

PART III: AWARENESS GENERATORS TO TRANSFORM UNMET NEEDS

INTRODUCTION

Returning to What Was Always Yours: The Journey from Unmet Needs to Wholeness

There's a concept we're going to explore in this book about the two different versions of us: an Essence version and a trained-in, fear-based defensive version. I believe it's of profound importance that each of us realizes we have these two different versions in us. Sounds a little wacky at first, but please hear me out.

You know when your partner or family member keeps getting stuck in the same pattern, and it's obvious to you, but they just can't see it? That's the two different versions of us in action. You know that person you were in a relationship with for the first six months to two years and now they've turned into a completely different person who doesn't like spontaneity anymore? That's the two different versions of us. (That last one might have a little bit too much of my own personal history in it. Giggle.)

Ever notice how someone under stress acts very differently from the way they behave when they're not? Yep, two versions. Ever notice how others habitually face unknowns compared to when the outcome is clear? Yeppers. Two versions. And lastly, ever notice how when you try to get this other person to see that they're stuck in repeating patterns, they can't see it? Their two versions haven't met each other yet.

This book is about bringing those two versions of us together. Because almost all of us have these two versions inside us now—we just don't know it because the fear-based defensive version is running through our unconscious processes. Meaning, it's hidden from our conscious awareness until we become aware of it.

This book is about becoming aware of the two different versions of you, compassionately, so that others don't have to try to keep getting you to see what you're doing that you don't know you're doing. Or, often more painfully, distance themselves from you without you understanding why.

Most of us carry wounds we don't consciously recognize, wounds formed not only from dramatic events but also from the quiet, on-going weighted absence of deeply important emotional needs. These unmet needs may seem subtle at first, but they quietly shape how we see ourselves, relate to others, and move through the world.

When these essential needs go unmet in childhood or later in life, we begin to disconnect from our authenticity, what I call our Essence. Without knowing why, we start to feel unworthy, unlovable, or inadequate. To protect ourselves from this pain, we develop internal defenses. These defenses were once helpful. They kept us safe. But now, they keep us distant from our wholeness.

This book is an invitation to come home to yourself . . . to your Essence.

Together, we'll explore a new understanding of why you feel the way you do, not as a flaw, but as a natural response to emotional needs that were never met. While it may seem like certain people or events caused your pain, the truth is more empowering: It began with the needs that weren't fulfilled, not with other people or with your worth. And the best part? This pattern of acting out or denying unmet needs can be transformed.

Through these pages, you'll learn to recognize unmet needs, re-connect with your internal resources, and meet those needs in real, lasting ways. You'll notice how your body quietly responds when it encounters a truth you've longed to feel. You'll begin to restore the parts of yourself that were never broken, only hidden.

Here are just some of the essential needs that, when fulfilled, restore us to wholeness:

- The felt sense of being inherently good and safe
- A deep connection between mind and body
- Trust in your inner knowing
- Validation of your internal experience
- A sense of belonging exactly as you are
- Emotional and nervous system regulation
- Empowerment in your ability to choose
- Joy in your natural creativity
- The strength to face uncertainty
- Authentic emotional connection and relational safety
- Being deeply known, seen, and valued
- Appreciation for your unique essence
- Trust in your presence to transform experience
- The right to feel good in your body as part of your worthiness to thrive

When these needs go unmet, they shape our personalities, behaviors, and emotional responses, not because something is wrong with us, but because something vital has been missing. Often, this absence wasn't intentional. Most of our caregivers didn't receive what they needed either. These patterns have been unconsciously passed down for generations. Now, we have a chance to break the cycle.

What You'll Discover in This Book

By the end of this book, you will be able to:

- Reconnect with your inner truth and know what you genuinely want
- Transform painful internal states into grounded, empowered presence
- Calm emotional and nervous system responses through self-awareness
- Express emotions in a way that creates connection instead of distance
- Understand and release old defense patterns that block authenticity
- Build emotional intimacy first with yourself, then with others
- Cultivate a life guided not by fear or lack, but by Essence and wholeness

This journey isn't about becoming someone new. It's about returning to who you've always been beneath the layers of the adaptations you made to survive. It's about remembering your Essence and learning how to live from it again.

My Road Back to Essence:
The Bicycle Wheel of Awareness

About fifteen years ago, I made a simple commitment: Whenever possible, I would ride my bike instead of driving. At first, I just wanted the exercise. But something unexpected happened. My intention evolved. Soon it wasn't only about movement; it was about the planet. Then something deeper emerged: a longing to experience the natural world more intimately. Today, it's all of those things and more.

To my surprise, my most meaningful contribution to the planet didn't come from biking. It came from transforming my internal world.

Even in a city of concrete and fast-moving metal, I began uncovering pockets of green life, trees stretching for light, insects buzzing with purpose, birds painting the sky with motion. There was still wonder to be found. I planted an intention in my unconscious mind: Notice nature. And it worked. Time and again, my head would instinctively turn toward something beautiful I might have missed without my unconscious priming to notice it.

I stitched together my own "green commute" through parks, down bike paths, and along greenbelts, a corridor of nature within the concrete city. But even more powerful than the route was the inner shift it sparked. Movement, intention, and connection with nature transformed how I experienced the world and myself.

Before this shift, my experience looked very different.

I saw myself as a victim of cars and drivers. They were my villains. They were rude, distracted, and dangerous. I was the righteous cyclist, trying to survive. When nearly hit, I'd fume with frustration. Those zoned-out, assumption-making drivers were the problem. Powerless, I fought back with fighty anger, my only available form of strength at the time.

My gestures screamed, *What are you doing? Don't you see me?* Not surprisingly, this didn't resolve anything. Drivers sped off defensively, and I rode away with a tight chest, replaying the scene. I couldn't slam a door on a bike, but I could slam the door of my heart.

What I hadn't yet realized:

- My mind and body needed to be in communication to feel whole.
- Unexamined emotions could fuse with my identity and overwhelm me.
- I had defensive ways of coping that hijacked my true self.
- My value wasn't conditional or external; it lived within me.
- Others' projections had more to do with their pain than with my worth.
- I hadn't yet learned to trust my Essence.

So, I made a deeper commitment to uncover it. I studied marriage and family therapy, became a therapist, and spent almost three decades helping myself and others move from defensive and afraid to present and empowered. I wanted an alternative to the automatic analysis of who's right and who's wrong. I wanted to know what was underneath the pain. I wanted to understand what made people feel unworthy, unlovable, or lost, and how to return them to themselves.

Evolution of the Ideas in This Book

When I was getting my master of fine arts degree, I wrote my thesis on *The Inner Game of Tennis* by W. Timothy Gallwey, repurposing it for acting/drama. I was fascinated with the concept of a Self 1 (the mind) telling a Self 2 (the body) what to do. It was my first understanding of what I intuitively knew. There are different versions of us inside, competing to be us. While I never became a great actor, I can recall a few sublime moments of brilliance where my mind and body were in sync with my Essence while acting.

My next big revelation came when I read Michael A. Singer's book *The Untethered Soul.* Singer's brilliant insight, that we have an observing awareness inside of us that can watch what we do, blew my mind as a concept and blew my experience wide open when I first felt it for myself. The empowerment of feeling one's sense of self outside the body's reexperiencing of unmet emotional pain (unmet needs) is something I want everyone to have. It's life-changing!

Dan Siegel's Wheel of Awareness expanded my skills in learning to identify with my observing awareness. I transformed his concepts into the Bicycle Wheel of Awareness (of course) and added some of my own concepts. When I imagine my sense of self at the hub of the wheel and my thoughts, feelings, body sensations, and perceptions at the rim of the wheel, this unique perspective shifts my internal states immediately. The feelings are not so overwhelming. My scary thoughts are not so believable. And my bodily sensations of pain can be clarified as memories of past emotional pain or current physical pain. (See "Observing Awareness" in Chapter 2.)

The next big leap of awareness I had about how our internal worlds really work was when I was riding my bike through an old-school shopping district in my city. We had green bike and car share lanes. Nothing could go wrong there. I was riding along with some parallel-parked cars on my right when I saw a big white object coming fast from my left. It was a car moving right at me. I thought, *I wonder if I can lift my legs high enough to keep them from being crushed between a parked car and this speeding car.*

Literally right at the last possible moment before contact, the white car swerved back the other way. Since my family taught me to get fighty angry when I'm afraid, the fighty anger burst out of me before I could consciously control it. I was yelling at the driver, "You almost killed me in your big metal car!" I hadn't noticed that the driver was staring at me through the sunroof. He began to blast me with way worse than I had offered him. He called me every allegedly derogatory thing he could think to call a woman and claimed he was the victim of some other guy almost running into him.

I go habitually quiet when someone's anger is greater than mine. We both, unfortunately, were stuck at a red light together. I was already planning on pulling over and getting some milk at the small convenience store right there and thought he would drive on. He did not. I got off my bike and noticed he had pulled over about thirty feet ahead. I grabbed my phone from my basket and pulled up 911, ready to call it, but waited . . . He was still walking toward me, yelling, but then he walked by me into the convenience store.

I unconsciously followed him in, reengaging in our fight for victimhood. The woman behind the counter started yelling at us to stop yelling. It was a messy display of reactivity. Then a man emerged from the other side of the one-aisle store and confronted my personal terrorist: "Dude, I saw what happened, and you did almost kill her." Then my personal terrorist started unloading on *that* guy.

What was most interesting, though, was what happened to my

insides. As soon as my other-side-of-the-store-aisle guy validated me, everything inside me settled. I no longer felt any driving impulse to get my personal terrorist to acknowledge he scared me. The incident was complete for me. My mind was no longer hooked. My body was no longer responding to an adrenaline alert. I dropped into a distilled presence and could now notice all the things around me.

Just then, a man walked into the small store and looked me in the eye and said, "Excuse me, ma'am. I saw what happened. Are you okay?" I said yes, and he said, "I will stand right here in case you need anything." I began to cry. I had been validated twice in a short period of time in ways that touched me deeply.

My personal terrorist went rushing by with his lottery tickets in hand. Good luck with that karma, Mr. Big Voice.

I had felt the power of Validation. It transformed my inner mind/body state from a sense-of-self alert mode and fighting to be right, to being resourced in my power, playfulness, curiosity, autonomy, and all my other Essence qualities. Instead of being right, I could just be me and let go of trying to control others. As I began using Validations with my clients, I realized it's the thing we are all trying to get from each other. The parts of each of us that didn't get validated, our trained-in powerlessness to feel worthy and lovable, need to be validated to transform.

The last and biggest puzzle piece to fall into place was about powerlessness. I had been using Karpman's Drama Triangle with clients for many years and had great success helping others move out of a victim mentality into an empowered mentality. The Drama Triangle has Victim, Villain, and Hero at its apexes.* Meaning, we move around the Drama Triangle playing the various roles of Victim, Villain, and Hero with each other when there's conflict or stress. I couldn't ever quite reconcile that every time we were the Villain or Hero, we were the

---

*One of my mentors, Kathlyn Hendricks began a body intelligence exploration of Karpman's drama triangle in the 1990s and changed persecutor to villain and rescuer to hero, to both modernize and de-Latinate these extremely useful roles so clients could play more readily.

Victim also. It finally occurred to me that it's not a triangle but a Stack of powerlessness, with Hero (Pleaser) and Villain (Punisher) defensive strategies erupting from our Victim powerlessness.

Our powerlessness, our claim to victimhood, is an attempt to get our need to know that we are good humans met. Remember my who's-right-who's-wrong battle with my personal terrorist? We were both fighting for our rightness, our need to know we are good and not the wrong one. As soon as I was validated, I no longer needed to be right and dropped into a deeper version of myself outside of right or wrong: my Essence. My powerlessness was transformed.

I now had the formula to Transform Victim powerlessness and unmet needs: By becoming the observing awareness, we could validate the parts of ourselves that did not get validated. The parts of us that didn't get validated are what imprinted our Victim powerlessness in the first place. What parts of us didn't get validated? Our feelings. Our feelings not being validated became our unmet needs, which rendered us feeling powerless of being lovable and worthy of getting our needs met. Powerlessness—the intense sense-of-self body sensations of the pain of an unmet need—transforms when validated, revealing the truth of who we are. I have been facilitating transformations with clients in my practice with great success. Now it was time for the world to know about the power of transforming. This book is the pathway to your transformation.

This Book Is the Inner Map

This book is the culmination of my discoveries about authenticity, the sense of self, powerlessness, defenses, Validations, and Simple Truth-telling. You'll learn more about all these here. It offers insights, tools, and pathways to transform fear, defensiveness, and reactivity into presence, power, and purpose. It will help you access your Essence, the creative, resilient, inner-peaceful part of you that's always been there.

So, what is Essence?

Essence is the part of you that is naturally whole. It's your inner safety and goodness, your capacity to meet life with curiosity instead of fear. It's the part of you that doesn't take things personally and responds with creativity instead of reactivity. Essence knows you belong just as you are. It's your connection to something larger, whether you call that life, love, God, or the universe.

When you live from Essence, you respond instead of reacting. You create instead of collapsing. You transform instead of defending. Most importantly, you remember you are already enough.

So, why don't we live from Essence all the time?

Because old strategies take over. Defenses hijack us. We react from wounds and avoid vulnerability. We protect ourselves from imagined threats and disconnect from what's real.

But transformation is possible. And it begins within.

The Heart of This Book

This book's core message is simple but powerful: Transformation is an inside job. Through guided Validations and internal actions, you'll learn to shift your inner landscape from fear and reactivity to clarity and Essence.

You'll discover how to:

- Reconnect with your body and inner truth
- Shift from powerlessness to personal agency
- Disentangle from defenses and reclaim authenticity
- Build emotional safety and resilience
- Create deeply connected relationships
- Speak to yourself internally from your Essence voice

My bike rides continue. But they feel different now. When something goes wrong, like a driver cutting me off, I don't reach for old habits of anger. I meet the moment with awareness and curiosity. And something surprising happens: Drivers stop to apologize. They wave me forward. They tap their chest and say, *That was on me.*

And every time, my body lights up with gratitude.

That's the power of inner transformation. It changes your world from the inside out.

Welcome to the ride. Welcome back to your Essence.

PART I

Get to Know Your Insides

A Gentle Note to the Reader

If you notice a deeply unpleasant feeling of draining energy in your body, it's likely something you've been trying not to feel for a long time—that's powerlessness. It takes effort to push feelings away. But here's the good news: You can transform them instead. What you're feeling isn't who you are; it's just a moment in time, an experience. When you bring kindness and curiosity to it, the feeling opens and softens. It just needs to know that it's allowed to be there and that someone cares about it.

As you read this book, you're teaching yourself how to trust your own ability to face and transform difficult sensations and emotions, instead of resisting or avoiding them.

If something stirs up discomfort within us as sadness, hopelessness, helplessness, or powerlessness, it's easy to blame someone else or even this book for bringing it back up in you. But those feelings were already in you. If you really think about it, you've been carrying them with you wherever you go. They can haunt you. Here's your opportunity to notice them, validate them, and transform them into ease and regulation.

There's so much realness and strength inside you, waiting to be seen and believed in. It's been hidden under old beliefs about powerlessness. It's time to free it.

If you miss the carefree part of yourself, the one who faces challenges without stress, who knows how to let go and experience daily joy, know this: It's still in you. The only thing blocking it is the belief that you are powerless. When you transform that belief, you reconnect with flow, ease, and joy. These Essence qualities are your authenticity.

Your relationship with your inner world—your feelings, sensations, and body cues—is the foundation of all your relationships. Strengthening this connection changes everything. Our culture has taught us to look for external solutions by taking external actions to try to change things. This book guides you into your internal actions to create change. It will feel weird at first even while a part of you senses that you're on the right track.

Inside you is courage, resilience, and a deep spark that knows how to lead the parts of you that feel powerless. You can meet those parts with strength and compassion. That's how transformation happens.

Your authenticity, the real you, comes alive when you reconnect with your inner Essence. Facing and transforming old beliefs about powerlessness is how you reclaim that connection. This is how you come back to your aliveness.

As you read, notice the meanings your mind creates. It might say, *I don't have time, This won't work,* or *I don't want to feel this.* These are familiar defenses, not the truth. What we're up to here is learning to trust our Essence, and to use the power of Validation to transform what once felt stuck.

If nonfiction feels hard to read, treat this book like a novel about you. Let your life, your memories, and your insights move through the pages. This is a book about being with your full experience, not just the easy parts. There is room in your authenticity for all of it.

Turning your attention inward was always meant to be an empowering act. At first it may feel hard because you're reaching into stuck or unmet parts of you. But once you realize those parts can transform, it's no longer so scary.

Meeting powerlessness with your Essence will surprise you. When you validate why a part of you feels powerless, you give it the power it needs to change. Those unmet parts aren't broken; they're waiting for you to meet them with loving care. When you do, they return you to who you truly are.

Your authenticity is the part of you that gets to relax and just be. It's the version of you that's connected to your inner truth, not dependent on external approval or identity. You can still enjoy outside support, but it no longer defines you. The time is now for you to enjoy your authenticity and everything you can create from it. You start by bringing authenticity to the parts of you that don't know how to be authentic yet.

CHAPTER 1

Two Versions of Us

"The way you see people is the way you treat them,
and the way you treat them is what they become."

—Goethe

This book's basic premise is that trained-in powerlessness is causing most humans to behave in defensive ways that are outside of their core values. Powerlessness can call to mind thoughts and words like *not good enough, unlovable, failure, incapable, unworthy,* and *unheard, unseen,* and *unknown.* Core values include kindness, compassion, empowerment, co-creating, resilience, lovingness, and thriving.

Even our people-pleasing defensive strategies are functioning outside of our core values because our inner people-pleaser feels powerless about being accepted if authentic. These defensive strategies, which I categorize as Pleasers, Protectors, and Punishers, require us to behave in inauthentic ways. These defensive strategies weren't taught to trust our inner power resources, our Essence qualities—empathy, curiosity, openness, courage, trust, flexibility, truth, and all the core values mentioned above.

How do we become more authentic? By teaching our powerlessness and our defensive strategies how to reconnect with our inner Essence qualities. This book unlocks this very process, allowing you to transform. Time to get into it.

Take a Moment to Choose This Moment

As we dive into this chapter, recall that transformation begins with internal awareness. We're learning to move from reacting defensively to responding with our authentic Essence. This chapter orients us to the foundational principles of this inner journey. Your defensive strategies think more external information is the way to have the new experience. Your Essence knows that having the creative experience first creates a totally new information stream from within, which is the truth. This book is about understanding the concepts by letting yourself learn experientially. So, do the exercises, dagnabbit! (Giggle.)

One day, I had a realization: I got angry because I was afraid. Remember the bike story? I recognized this truth when I found myself retaliating against drivers who scared me while I was riding. They'd shout insults or flip me off, and I'd react with outrage. But something wasn't working. I wasn't getting the result I wanted. I wanted them to self-reflect, to do something different this time and the next time.

So, I began experimenting. What kind of reaction from me would get the outcome I wanted? The surprising answer was authenticity and compassion. I know: How was I supposed to give kindness to someone who didn't "deserve" it? But I ran the experiment anyway. The first time I waved with understanding instead of flailing dramatically, the driver *rolled down their window and apologized.* Bing-bammo! I kept it up, and the more compassionate I became, the more drivers self-reflected. The angry version of me got more conflict; the compassionate version got connection and apologies!

Once, shortly after that, a therapy client of mine cut me off in traffic. I didn't realize it was them until after I offered my kind wave. Bam-o-whammo! If I hadn't, that could have been my *ex*-client.

Simple Truth: If we can see others' two versions but not our own, we're not looking closely enough.

Essence Mode and Defensive Mode and the Who's-Right-Who's-Wrong System

At the core, there are only two ways of being in any moment: open to learning from what's happening (Essence mode) or closed to it (defensive mode). We are open to learning when we feel understood. We are closed to learning when we feel evaluated as right or wrong. Defensive strategies assess rightness or wrongness while Essence sees, speaks, and acts from truth.

The who's-right-who's-wrong version of trying to get to the truth about how to be a good human comes from our defensive strategies' version of the truth. Defensive strategies work hard to get our needs met so we can feel like good people without knowing how to access our internal Essence qualities. So, our defensive strategies don't know how to trust our inner truth as a bodily felt experience. Defensive strategies try to impose external right or wrong rules onto the self and others as the right way to do things. Our Essence senses the truth from deep within and acts from this truth.

Defense vs. Essence Physiologies

DEFENSIVE MODE

Head and Body Working
Against Each Other

ESSENCE MODE

Head and Body Working
Together to Thrive

Pseudo-power
efforting, trying harder,
resisting, forcing

Powerlessness
covered by defenses,
judgment, control,
"better than"

SENSATIONS
tightness pulling up,
holding together,
heaviness, draining down

EMOTIONS
shame, sadness, fear,
hopeless, helpless,
powerless

Grounded and enlivened
(settled energy)

Authentic power and
clarity of the whole
picture

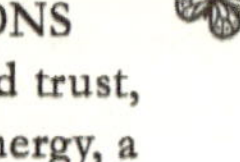

SENSATIONS
inner safety and trust,
free-flowing energy, a
calm, grounded presence

EMOTIONS
enthusiastic readiness,
love and joy flowing
naturally

In the previous graphic, notice how our mind and body states can lead to an empowered or a disempowered condition. Our perceptions of our own emotions, our self, others, and the world shift dramatically depending on our internal physical and mental states.

When you're feeling creative, curious, and authentic, you're open to learning. You feel alive and naturally want to connect with others. Your nervous system sends a signal of safety, helping others feel safe and open around you. This physiological state fosters deep, nourishing connection and joy.

When we're open to learning, we already feel how we want to feel. We don't reach outside ourselves to feel better. Even ordinary moments can feel like magical discoveries. Problems can be resolved clearly and fully. There's no need for blame, so connection remains intact even during conflict. This is Essence.

Our Essence is packed with qualities that convey our inherent goodness

Loving kindness, present-moment awareness, moment-to-moment creativity, aliveness, authenticity, flexibility, curiosity, courage, worthiness, and inner safety are all ways we can get our needs met and feel good about it.

In Essence, we're whole. We act from internal abundance rather than lack. The need to prove ourselves disappears. Instead, we cocreate reality, taking what's here, adding our own creative spark, and bringing something new into being. See the full list of Essence qualities on the next page.

Essence Qualities List

Absorption	Captivating	Decisiveness	Facilitating
Abundance	Caring	Dedicating	Facing
Accepting	Celebrating	Deepening	Fairness
Accessibility	Changeability	Delighting	Faithfulness
Accomplishing	Cheerfulness	Dependability	Feeling
Accountability	Cherishing	Desiring	Fidelity
Adaptability	Choosing	Determination	Flexibility
Adherence	Clarity	Devoting	Flowing
Adventuring	Clear	Dignifying	Fluidity
Affection	Cleverness	Diligence	Focusing
Agency	Cohering	Directness	Fondness
Alacrity	Collaborating	Discerning	Forgiving
Alertness	Comforting	Discipline	Fortitude
Aligning	Committing	Discretion	Freedom
Aliveness	Communicating	Drive	Freshness
All-ness	Communion	Dynamic	Friendliness
Allowing	Community	Eagerness	Generating
Alluring	Companioning	Easeful	Generosity
Altruism	Compassion	Ecstasy	Genius-ing
Ambition	Competency	Efficaciousness	Gentleness
Appreciating	Completing	Efficiency-ing	Giddiness
Asserting	Composure	Effulgence	Giggling
Assiduousness	Concise	Electrifying	Giving
Assuring	Concordance	Elucidating	Goodness
Attending	Confidence	Embodying	Graciousness
Attuning	Confidentiality	Embracing	Gratifying
Authenticity	Congruity	Emergence	Gratitude
Autonomy	Connecting	Empathizing	Grounding
Availability	Conscious-ing	Encouraging	Growing
Avidness	Consenting	Endurance	Harmonizing
Awesomeness	Considering	Energizing	Healing
Balancing	Consistency	Engaging	Helpfulness
Beauty	Contemplating	Engendering	Honesty
Becoming	Contentment	Enlivening	Honoring
Befriending	Contributing	Enthusing	Hoping
Belonging	Conviction	Equality	Hospitality
Benevolence	Cooperating	Equanimity	Humbleness
Blissing	Courage	Ethicalness	Humor
Boldness	Courtesy	Evoking	Illuminating
Both/And-ing	Creativity	Evolving	Imagining
Bravery	(moment-moment)	Exciting	Immersing
Buoyancy	Credible	Exhilarating	Impacting
Calmness	Curiosity	Expectancy	Independence
Candor	Dancing	Exploring	Individuating
Capability	Daring	Expressing	Industriousness

Essence Qualities List

Ingenuity	Meaning	Realizing	Subtleness
Initiating	Meditating	Receiving	Suppleness
Innocence	Mentoring	Reconciliation	Supporting
Innovating	Mercy	Recreating	Surprising
Inquisitive	Mindfulness	Redemption	Surrendering
Insight	Miracle-ing	Reflecting	Sustainability
Inspiring	Mirthfulness	Reframing	Sympathy
Instinct	Mobility	Reifying	Synthesis
Integrating	Modeling	Relaxing	Tactfulness
Integrity	Moving	Releasing	Teaching
Intelligence	Multiculturalism	Reliability	Tenaciousness
Intentness	Nimbleness	Relishing	Tenderness
Inter-reliance-ing	Nonattachment	Repairing	Thoroughness
Interest	Noticing	Replenishing	Thoughtfulness
Interesting	Nourishing	Resoluteness	Thriving
Intervening	Nuancing	Resolving	Timelessness
Intriguing	Numinous	Resourcing	Tranquility
Intuiting	Nurturing	Respecting	Transcending
Inventing	Omniscience	Responsibility	Transforming
Invigorating	Oneness	Responsiveness	Trusting
Invoking	Openness	Revealing	Truthfulness
Joining	Ordering	Reverence	Unconditional-loving
Joviality	Organicity	Sacredness	Understanding
Joying	Organizing	Securing	Unifying
Justice	Orienting	Sensitivity	Uniqueness
Keenness	Originality	Sensuality	Universality
Kindness	Passion	Serendipity	Valiantness
Knowing	Patience	Service	Validating
Leading	Pausing	Sexuality	Valor
Liberating	Peace	Sharing	Visioning
Liberty	Permeability	Silence	Vivaciousness
Lightness	Persistence	Simplifying	Warmth
Liminal	Playfulness	Sincerity	Welcoming
Listening	Pliableness	Softening	Wholeness
Love	Power	Solitude	Willingness
Loving	Practicing	Soothing	Wisdom
Loyalty	Preparedness	Spaciousness	Within-ness
Lucidity	Presence-ing	Sparkling	Wondering
Magnifying	Privacy	Special-ing	Worthiness
Majesty	Prosperity	Spirituality	
Manifesting	Purifying	Spontaneity	
Marveling	Purposefulness	Steadfastness	
Mastering	Quality	Stewarding	
Matching	Radiance	Strengthening	
Mattering	Readiness	Structuring	

This list reveals all the resources you have inside of you to create your experiences—over 350 amazing resources already in you. Notice how many of them are warm and fuzzy qualities and how many of them are "gettin' things done" qualities.

When we're closed to learning, we're defending ourselves. Our behaviors come from unconscious beliefs that say something is wrong with us—or the world—and we must act a certain way to be safe. This is defensive mode, and the behaviors that arise from it are defensive strategies. Even our confidence is different depending on whether we're in powerlessness—employing defensive strategies of the Pleaser, Protector, or Punisher—or in Essence. Check out the graphic on the following page.

Notice all the different types within each category. Circle the ones you can recognize in yourself. Challenge yourself to look at the ones that are hard for you to own because you are remembering you are learning to transform them.

We've all learned defensive strategies to get our needs met. They're built on the idea that we'll be accepted if we show up the "right" way and shunned if we don't. Being shunned feels like being rejected at our core. In defensive mode, we try to avoid what we fear instead of creating what we desire.

Defensive mode is about *managing* internal discomfort rather than *experiencing* it. When we avoid sadness, react angrily to fear, or distract ourselves from pain, we're defending. Withdrawal, attack, distraction—these are all defenses. The way we learn to attach to others is often through defenses and powerlessness instead of Essence.

Types of Pleasers, Protectors, Punishers, and Victim Powerlessness

Pleasers, Protectors, and Punishers use *active strategies* to manage safety, value, and connection (even if unconscious or maladaptive). Victim Powerlessness is not an active strategy. It is a *state of giving up or collapse.*

Strategies of Pleasers

Action	Identity-Shifting	Manipulating	Avoidance
Rescuer	Charmer	White Liars	Can't-Say-No
Hero	Chameleon	Playing the Victim	Being "Nice" at
Savior	Super-Agreeable	Martyr	All Costs
Sacrificer	Needless	Sufferer	Settler
"I'll do it for you"	Appeaser	Woe-Is-Me-er	Enmesher
Overcomer	Super-Sweet	Assume-er	Stay-Busy-er
Striver	Super	Minimizer	Distractor
Over-Scheduler	Compliment-er	Dopamine-	Pretender
Effort-er	Lover-Bombers	Chaser	Self-Needs
Over-Promiser	Non-Challenger	Externalizer	Devalue-er
	Turn-Coat-er		

Pleasers seek value and safety by gaining approval, avoiding conflict, and adapting to others' needs in order to feel worthy and accepted.

Strategies Protectors

Control-Oriented	Avoidance & Withdrawal	Acting Out	Manipulating or Identity-Defending
Controller	Invisible	Histrionic	Addict
Judger	Voiceless	Agitator	Distance-er
Perfectionist	Procrastinator	Rebel	Super-Consumer
Worrier	Ghoster	Incessant Talker	Liar
Super-Competent	Always Busy	Instigator	Intellectualizer
Skeptic	Rejector	Schemer	Confuse-er
Self-Righteous	Abandoner	Gossiper	Bad-Mouth-er
Idealizer	Passive-	Sarcastic	Deflector
Conspiracy	Aggressive	Cheater	Detach-er
Theorist	Grand Exit-er	Betrayer	
Grandiose	Fantisizer		

Protectors seek value and safety by staying in control and hiding their true self, believing this will keep them from getting hurt.

Strategies of Punishers

Overt Aggression	Verbal Attacking	Covert Manipulation	Withdrawal
Aggressor	Blamer	Manipulator	Withholder
Intimidator	Shamer	Denier	Withdrawer
Bully	Name-Caller	You Snooze, You Lose	Stonewaller
Corporal Punisher	Criticizer	No Pain, No Gain	Coldhearted
Criminal	Diminish-er	Bias-er	Dismiss-er
Troller	Retaliator	Stubborn	Disregard-er
Overpowerer	Backstabber	Close-Minded	Resent-er
Justifier	Curtness	Disapproving	Un-appreciator
	Should-er	Disappointed	Divider
	Intruder		

Punishers seek value and safety by controlling others and asserting superiority to avoid feeling powerless or vulnerable.

Expressions of Victim Powerlessness

Overwhelmed	Scarcity	Hopelessness	Self-Pity
Can't Do It.	There's not enough time, money, love, energy.	I'll never be happy.	Why should I even try?
It's Too Hard.		I'll always be alone.	What did I do to deserve this?
It's Too Much.	Unlucky	Nothing matters.	No one cares.
I'm Too Much.	Things never go my way.	It's always going to be like this.	After everything I've done for you.
I'm Not Enough.	No one understands me.		
Have-To-er			

Victim Powerlessness seeks value and safety by disclaiming responsibility and fault so others will step in and take more responsibility.

Some defensive strategies you may not have thought about

Managing others' reactions, efforting, minimizing, disappearing, fixing, deflecting, perfectionism, dreading, concealing, procrastinating, complaining, saying *I'm fine*, resenting, assuming, divisiveness, narcissism, rejecting, talking too much, moodiness, and using platitudes like "It is what it is." See the full list of defensive strategies:

Defensive Strategies List

Abandoning	Being incompetent	Cheating	Fainting
Abusing	Being inconsiderate	Close-mindedness	Fantasizing
Acting cool	Being indifferent	Coercing	Feeling superior
Acting out	Being inert	Cold-hearting	Feigning weakness
Acting out feelings	Being inhibited	Collapsing	Finding loopholes
Advice giving	Being irreverent	Concealing	Fixating
Always being right	Being lazy	Condemning	Fixing it
Agitating	Being messy	Condescending	Flattering
Analyzing	Being moody	Conditional loving	Forcing
Antipathy	Being narcissistic	Confounding	Forced conformity
Appropriating	Being negative	Confusing	Freezing
Assuming	Being nonchalant	Constraining	Gaslighting
Attacking	Being opinionated	Constricting	Getting rid of it
Backstabbing	Being oppositional	Contracting	Giving ultimatums
Being a coward	Being overconcerned	Controlling	Giving up
Being aggressive	Being overprotective	Corrupting	Gloominess
Being aloof	Being over-logical	Criticizing	Gossiping
Being ambiguous	Being passive	Critiquing	Guilting
Bing ambivalent	Being perfect	Deadening	Haphazard-ing
Being annoyed	Being perfunctory	Deceiving	Harshness
Being apathetic	Being pessimistic	Defending	Hiding
Being aversive	Being preoccupied	Deflecting	Hindering
Being bored	Being pretentious	Denying	Hoarding
Being callous	Being rigid	Detaching	Idealizing
Being careless	Being routine	Detesting	Ignoring
Being closed off	Being sarcastic	Devaluing	Impatience
Being competitive	Being self-righteous	Disapproving	Imposing your will
Being complacent	Being shortsighted	Disconnected	Indecisiveness
Being compulsive	Being submissive	Discounting	Intellectualizing
Being crude	Being supercompetent	Discouraging	Interfering
Being cruel	Being the strong one	Discriminating	Interrupting
Being curt	Being tuned out	Disengaging	Intimidating
Being cynical	Being unreasonable	Dismissing	Intolerant
Being demanding	Being vague	Disregarding	Judging

Defensive Strategies List

Being depressed	Belittling	Disrespecting	Justifying
Being disloyal	Betraying	Disrupting	Keeping busy
Being dissident	Bewilderment	Dissociating	Labeling
Being divisive	Biasing	Distracting	Labeling good or bad
Being flippant	Blaming	Downplaying	Lack of appreciation
Being frustrated	Bolstering	Dreading	Last word-ing
Being glib	Breaking down	Efforting	Lecturing
Being grandiose	Busying	Energy vampire-ing	Limiting
Being harried	Capitulating	Enmeshing	Lying
Being hyper-vigilant	Catastrophic thinking	Entitlement	Making excuses
Being impertinent	Championing	Externalizing	Making wrong
Manipulating	Pragmatism	Segregating	Supressing feelings
Meandering	Pretending	Self-absorption	Talking too much
Minimizing	Procrastinating	Self-doubting	Tantrum-ing
Misinterpreting	Projecting	Self-conceit	Underestimating
Moralizing	Rebuffing	Separating	Using contempt
Nagging	Rejecting	Seriousness	Using counter-will
Neglecting	Repeating	Settling	Using dissension
Numbing	Repressing	Shaming	Using platitudes
Obliviousness	Resenting	Shoulding	Vacillating
Obsessing	Resisting	Shutting down	Waffling either/or-ing
Omitting	Restricting	Sidestepping	Watching the clock
Overcompensating	Retaliating	Skewing information	Whining
Overconcern	Ridiculing	Snubbing	White knuckling
Overprotection	Rigid individualism	Splitting	White lying
Overreacting	Ruminating	Staying stuck	Withdrawing
Perfunctoriness	Sarcastic	Stonewalling	Withholding
Permissiveness	Scolding	Stressing	Worrying
Playing small	Second-guessing	Stubbornness	
Plea for approval	Secrecy	Submissiveness	
Possessiveness	Seeking approval	Superficiality	

When you take a look at the full list of defensive strategies, it explains a lot about how we treat each other when we experience ourselves as victims (powerlessness). When we transform our powerlessness, our defensive strategies transform back into their own authentic Essence.

Take a Moment to Choose This Moment

Reflect on how many of your actions today were moti-
vated by trying to change something outside of yourself
to feel better inside. How many came from internal
inspiration? Your defensive strategies can be softened
when met with Essence. Meet them with compassion
and curiosity. Imagine trying to feel loving without having access to your own loving Essence inside. This is the
stuck plight of our defensive strategies. Love becomes
performance. When we validate and appreciate our
defenses, though, they begin to relax us into a mind/
body state of being settled and balanced inside, where
we can feel our authentic loving presence.

Most of us don't realize how often we operate from defense. Venting, complaining, blaming, comparing—these are attempts to get our
needs met, albeit in disconnected ways. A key sign that a defensive
strategy is in play: the belief that not everyone can get their needs met.
Another key sign of defense: You can only see things from one perspective. One more key sign a defense is active in you, and you haven't
known it: You're not getting the results you want easily.

The Neuroscience of Nurturance

For years, scientists believed the amygdala was the emotional center of
the brain. We now know it's part of a broader emotional system. The
amygdala (the fear center) sits between the brain stem (the center of

instinctive reactions) and the prefrontal cortex (the center of rational thought and empathy).

When the prefrontal cortex is active, it soothes the amygdala. But when we enter defensive mode, it goes offline. For many of us, this disconnection is learned early and passed down through generations.

Allan Schore, super-smart neuroscientist, in *The Science of the Art of Psychotherapy* explains that memory consolidation integrates information through our autonomic nervous system first before it reaches other parts of the brain. The autonomic nervous system perceives threats to the body or the sense of self. If our autonomic nervous system was trained to perceive sense-of-self threats, most of our memories about who we are and whether we're lovable or worthy have fear trained into them instead of Essence.

This fear-based training happens from within the womb to around three years old. Because autobiographical memory doesn't come online until we're about three years old, we can be afraid and not know why, or we can use defensive strategies to shut down our fears, so we don't even know our sense of self comes from fear.

If our caregivers met our Essence with their own defenses, their nervous systems were not capable of soothing ours. Their discomfort taught us to shut down our emotional intuitions, the very function that would later have helped us regulate.

When the prefrontal cortex nurtures the amygdala, we feel settled, soothed, and calm. If our parents had met our fear with true compassion, they could have taught us how to self-soothe. Instead, we inherited their defensiveness as the way to regulate our feelings. You can see a visual of how this happens in the following two graphics.

Notice how devastating the defensive who's-right-who's-wrong attitude can be to our internal experience of ourselves. Our sense of self and body get imprinted with self-doubt and fear of doing it wrong.

How Truth Affects the
Sense of Self and Body

When a parent supports and validates a child's inner world, the child learns to value their own thoughts and feelings. This encourages them to trust their inner resources and feel connected to their natual sense of goodness, their Essence. Their sense of self and body function from Essence.

SENSE OF SELF

BODY

Essence

The internally validated child sees themselves as the one who gives value and creates meaning. They trust their inner truth to guide their actions.

Their sense of self is rooted in being an aware, transforming presence.

When a child's inner expereince is validated, they learn to see it as valuable, filled with inner resources and natural goodness.

Free-flowing energy, unguarded, no sense-of-self threat.

Wide range of feelings experienced from empowerment.

Feelings trigger, flourish, and settle in seconds.

Aliveness is experienced as desire to engage with life.

How "Wrong" Affects the
Sense of Self and Body

When a parent's being-right defensive strategies imprint wrongness/fear in the child's Essence, the child acts in ways that make the parent feel safe, even if it means hiding their real feelings. Their sense of self and body pay the price.

SENSE OF SELF

BODY

The child begins to believe that being "good" means pleasing or protecting others and ignoring what they feel inside, which leaves their true self ignored.

They learn that right and wrong come from outside of them, instead of from inner truth. They start to think their true self might be wrong.

Disconnected from their inner Essence, they rely on defensive strategies to feel safe and meet their needs.

Guarded
Heaviness
Tightness
Nausea
Shame
Fear
Emptiness
Collapsed
Always on alert
Contracted

STACK

On a Stack: Powerlessness, Pleasers, Protectors, and Punishers

Simple Truth: When we're "Stacked," we justify harm because we believe someone is blocking us from what we need, harming us.

The Stack

This is an internal depiction of our trained-in powerlessness and defensive strategies. Powerlessness fills the body as body sensations, and the sense of self gets pulled into this powerlessness believing it could be true. The Pleaser, Protector, and Punisher defensive strategies attempt to pull the energy of the human up and out of powerlessness into guarded actions. The Pleaser, Protector, and Punisher do the best they can to try and make the powerlessness go away. Yet, since the powerlessness doesn't transform using defensive strategies, it remains in full force to trigger the same way the next time. This is a stuck repeating pattern.

Notice in the graphic above how much our internal body can work against its own experience, resisting what's actually happening instead of validating it. We feel intense sensations of wrongness when Stacked that no one taught us how to deal with, so we go into a guarded stance to try to get ourselves out of it as fast as possible. Being on a Stack is a stuck and repeating body/mind state.

Being Stacked means having unprocessed experiences piled on top of each other. Our energy is whacked. Energy drains downward from powerlessness and gets pushed upward into defensive strategies. In this mind/body state, we are incapable of connecting to our internal Essence resources.

Victim powerlessness, the feeling that the sense of self is wrong—and therefore broken, bad, unlovable, unwanted, unworthy, failing, or inadequate—is a belief that can disconnect us from our Essence qualities. The Pleaser, Protector, and Punisher defensive strategies, learned from caretakers, kick in to try to get the Essence feeling back. Unfortunately, they have no pathways to Essence because they transact with the external world for Validation instead of feeling it from within.

We were trained to pull ourselves out of our feelings of powerlessness by adapting to the system of people-pleasing. We became a Pleaser, fusing our sense of self with how others see us. We develop Protectors to limit how we behave in order to be loved. When our Pleaser defensive strategies fail, it feels like we ourselves failed or are wrong. We crash into our own fighty-anger resentful Punisher defensive strategies with the sentiment *I can never do anything right! You never appreciate what I do!*

These strategies try to meet our needs but create unwanted side effects. Pleasers strive to be good by sacrificing the needs of the self. Unfortunately, our Pleasers need a certain kind and amount of appreciation, and if they don't get it, they slide into resentment. Protectors are trying hard to make sure we don't do anything wrong. Protectors limit us and others as the way to stay safe or feel powerful. Two important needs. Tragically, our Protectors activate rebellious defensive strategies in ourselves and others that require sabotage and subterfuge as the way to get needs met. No one loves sabotage or subterfuge. Punishers lash out when our needs go unmet. When the Pleaser face-plants into resentment, our Punishers rear up their dragon heads and retaliate by calling names, criticizing, or judging. Punishers feel adrenalized power in the moment, but as soon as the adrenaline wears off, it's apology time.

Let's dive a bit into a comparison of how these defensive strategies and Essence work inside of us. Notice how each one talks to us in our head, altering our different systems inside, such as our emotional system, attentional system, respiratory system, and sense-of-self system.

Confidence Strategies of the Pleaser

- Focuses on doing things for others to feel settled inside.
- Uses pleasing strategies as a way to feel unique or special.
- Distrusts the body and tries to manage it from the outside.
- Tries to protect the self from being judged, blamed, or rejected.
- Needs the outside world to go well in order to feel okay inside.
- Believes approval from others will lead to love, power, or worth.
- Disconnected from their own body, yet trying hard to make it feel better.
- Has an inner voice that says, *"You'll feel better if you just do this right now."*
- Borrows ideas, styles, or behaviors from others and presents them as their own.
- Main strategies: appeasing, pleasing, rescuing, perfecting, fixing, and pretending.
- Feels not good enough when strategies don't work and often shifts into blame or criticism.
- So focused on guarding the self, they miss true connection, first with themselves, then with others.

For a Pleaser, each of these behaviors is a way to manage discomfort, secure safety, or feel temporarily valued, all in hopes of accessing a feeling of confidence or worth. But because they're rooted in external approval, they cause conditional confidence. The moment approval is lost, or the strategy fails, that sense of confidence collapses.

Confidence Strategies of the Punisher

- Relies on comparisons to feel superior.
- Feels angry or disappointed when strategies fail.
- Needs the external world to confirm their worth.
- Motivates through threats, shame, or manipulation.
- Demands approval or punishes when it's not given.
- Uses control or criticism to feel powerful or unique.
- Avoids feeling pain in the body or gets consumed by it.
- Either avoids inner powerlessness or uses it to push for change.
- Focuses on outside actions to gain power, value, love, or security.
- Borrows traits or ideas from others and claims them as their own.

A Punisher tries to feel confident by controlling, criticizing, or overpowering others. They avoid feeling powerless by using threats, shame, or manipulation to get results. Their sense of worth depends on outside reactions, and when strategies fail, they often feel angry or disappointed, and their confidence collapses.

Confidence Strategies of the Powerless Victim

- Relies on others to take over tasks or make decisions.
- Believes their needs can't be met without outside help.
- Focuses on problems and obstacles instead of solutions.
- Equates safety with staying small, unseen, or dependent.
- Avoids responsibility to protect self from blame or failure.
- Uses self-doubt, hopelessness, or overwhelm to avoid action.
- Feels powerless when facing challenges and withdraws from effort.
- Uses sympathy or rescue from others as a source of value or connection.
- Uses "why try" thinking to lower expectations and avoid disappointment.
- Gains a sense of worth by recruiting others to take responsibility for what they could take responsibility for.

A Victim tries to feel safe and valued by appearing unable or at a disadvantage. They rely on others to take over or make decisions, believing their needs can't be met on their own. Confidence depends on being rescued or receiving sympathy, and when help doesn't come, they often feel hopeless, withdraw, or stop trying. Victim Powerlessness can build true confidence by turning fear-based "have to" or "no choice" habits into the empowered confidence of owning their choices.

Confidence Strategies of the Protector

- Keeps emotions and vulnerabilities hidden to maintain control.
- May distance from others to prevent being hurt or disappointed.
- Seeks security by managing outcomes and reducing unpredictability.
- Feels uneasy when not in control or when boundaries are challenged.
- Relies on planning, perfectionism, or withdrawal to manage uncertainty.
- Avoids risks and new experiences that might challenge the sense of safety.
- Gains a sense of safety and worth by limiting exposure to perceived threats.
- Uses caution, rules, or boundaries to guard the self from harm or judgment.
- Focuses on controlling situations or people to prevent mistakes or being wrong.
- Prioritizes self-protection over openness, which can limit connection with self and others.

A Protector tries to feel confident by controlling situations and avoiding risks, hoping this will keep them safe. They look outside themselves to calm inner fears, depending on the world to feel steady and predictable. This focus on control can unintentionally block deeper connection with themselves and others. With practice, Protectors can learn to find safety and confidence from within instead of from the outside.

Essence-Manifesting Strategies

- Sources confidence and power from within.
- Connects mind and body to access inner resources.
- Creates new, authentic ideas, movements, and expressions.
- Finds uniqueness in inner qualities rather than external validation.
- Prioritizes learning, connection, growth, love, and creating goodness.
- Guided by an inner voice that speaks Simple Truths and sparks creativity.
- Leads with openness, deepening authentic connections with self and others.
- Sees no threats to the self and trusts in the ability to work through challenges.
- Enjoys connection with the body and can transform discomfort into ease and flow.
- Sees Essence in self and others even when powerlessness and defenses are activated.

Essence gains confidence from within, drawing on an inner connection between mind and body. Guided by Simple Truths, it creates authentic ideas and transforms discomfort into ease and flow. Confidence is steady because it's not dependent on outside approval, allowing openness, creativity, and genuine connection with self and others.

Notice all the different ways we try to feel like who we are. In Essence, we resource our confidence and value from our inner Essence resources. In powerlessness, fear, and defense, we source our confidence and value from an external source.

Transforming Victim powerlessness back to Essence internally dissolves the need for Pleaser, Protector, and Punisher defensive strategies, allowing them to reconnect with their organic roles in Essence.

Body Sensations

Avoiding emotions often comes down to avoiding sensations like heaviness, emptiness, numbness, or chaos. These sensations make us feel fundamentally wrong. Because we aren't taught to separate our sense of self from our feelings, we believe we *are* our feelings. Blocking sensations makes them stuck.

Learning to validate your bodily sensations instead of avoiding them or acting them out is how to return to Essence *tout suite*.

We constantly shift between Essence and defense, often without noticing. To track these shifts, we need to reconnect with our bodies. The world looks different depending on which version of us is present.

Simple Truth: In Essence, we create harmony. In defense, we often cause harm.

The graphic on the following page demonstrates how we can distort reality when looking through powerlessness, fear, and defenses compared to Essence. It's super-weird to think of our mind distorting reality! It does this by limiting our perception, so we interpret what's happening through our trained-in fear. This is how we take things personally. Inserting our sense of self-worth and lovability into the

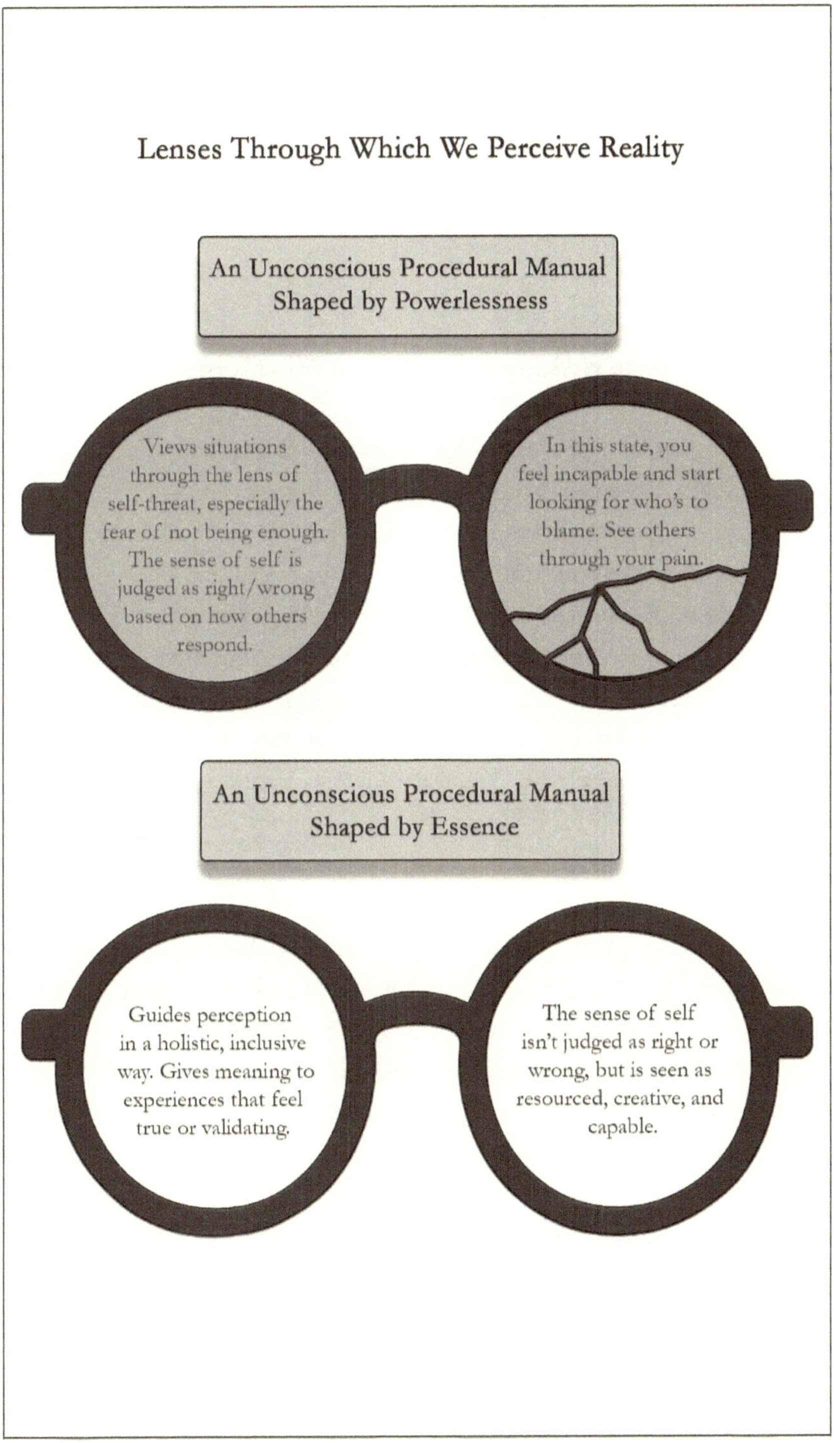
Lenses Through Which We Perceive Reality
An Unconscious Procedural Manual Shaped by Powerlessness
Views situations through the lens of self-threat, especially the fear of not being enough. The sense of self is judged as right/wrong based on how others respond.
In this state, you feel incapable and start looking for who's to blame. See others through your pain.
An Unconscious Procedural Manual Shaped by Essence
Guides perception in a holistic, inclusive way. Gives meaning to experiences that feel true or validating.
The sense of self isn't judged as right or wrong, but is seen as resourced, creative, and capable.

meanings we give: If someone is seeing me as bad, maybe I really am bad. Notice how someone only sees someone else as bad if they are looking through their own lens of victim powerlessness and thereby needing a villain. Such vicious cycles of fear we're capable of unconsciously running on each other.

Take a Moment to Choose This Moment

Notice how your body responds as you read the following Essence qualities: safety, openness, flow, connection, creativity, authenticity, and curiosity. Now notice how your body responds as you read these defensive strategies: blame, judgment, withdrawal, rigidity, control, and dismissing. Feel the difference? You just felt the two different versions of you. When we're in Essence, we're open to learning. When we're in defense, we're closed. You can feel this in your body.

The Feeling Cycle graphic defines some of these sensations. Trigger is when you notice the body sensations of feelings. Flourish is when the feelings hit their peak of intensity experientially. Settle is the return to a baseline of experience without the previously felt feeling. Many of us were unintentionally taught to have dysregulated emotions and nervous systems. Dysregulation sends us into alert mode, where we start thinking, acting, or choosing on the flourish of our feelings (as body sensations). Regulated emotional and nervous systems pause to validate on the flourish, so settling happens before thinking, acting, or choosing. For example, we're angry and we want to lash out because we're believing our fears stories would be a validation to express to the self to settle the flourish.

The Feeling Cycle
Body Sensations of Triggering, Flourishing, and Settling

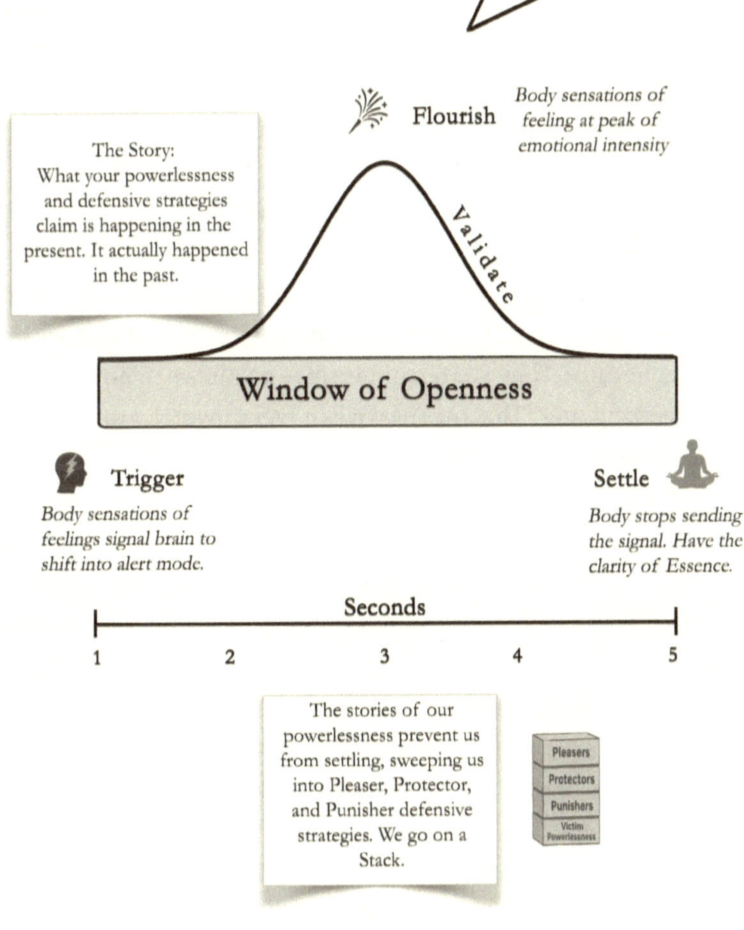

Where do we think or act from when dysregulated? Our own fear-based perspectives, which are filtered through our powerlessness beliefs. The flourish of body sensations we feel while having a powerlessness belief can engulf our sense of self in past pain so we're not sure whether it is happening in the present moment. For example, if my powerlessness belief is that I'm weak or stupid if I make a mistake, then while I'm in the flourish phase of the feeling cycle, I will believe that others are seeing me as stupid or weak when I make a mistake or falter in my solutions. I may accuse them of doing so whether that was their intention or not. I'm seeing them through my own powerlessness belief of fear.

Powerlessness Beliefs

Powerlessness beliefs are unconscious thoughts that limit us and disconnect us from our worth. They accompany body sensations we don't want to feel because they stem from unmet needs we're not sure we're worthy of getting met. This means we can feel unworthy of having our needs met because they didn't get met.

It's easy to understand how so many needs went unmet when you consider how no one really knows how to validate each other. If needs aren't validated, powerlessness beliefs are formed. Check out the Feeling Cycle graphic on the next page to see how powerlessness beliefs intensify and prolong feelings because they hold a threat of unworthiness to get a need met.

Notice how we can give meaning to what's happening that enmeshes our sense of self into what's happening. We activate our own threat alert modes with our powerlessness beliefs. Our threat alert mode interrupts our natural feeling cycle of trigger, flourish, and settle.

Some common powerlessness beliefs include:

- *If things go wrong, I'm a failure.*
- *If someone leaves me, I'm unlovable.*

The Feeling Cycle
Interrupted by Powerlessness Beliefs and Stories

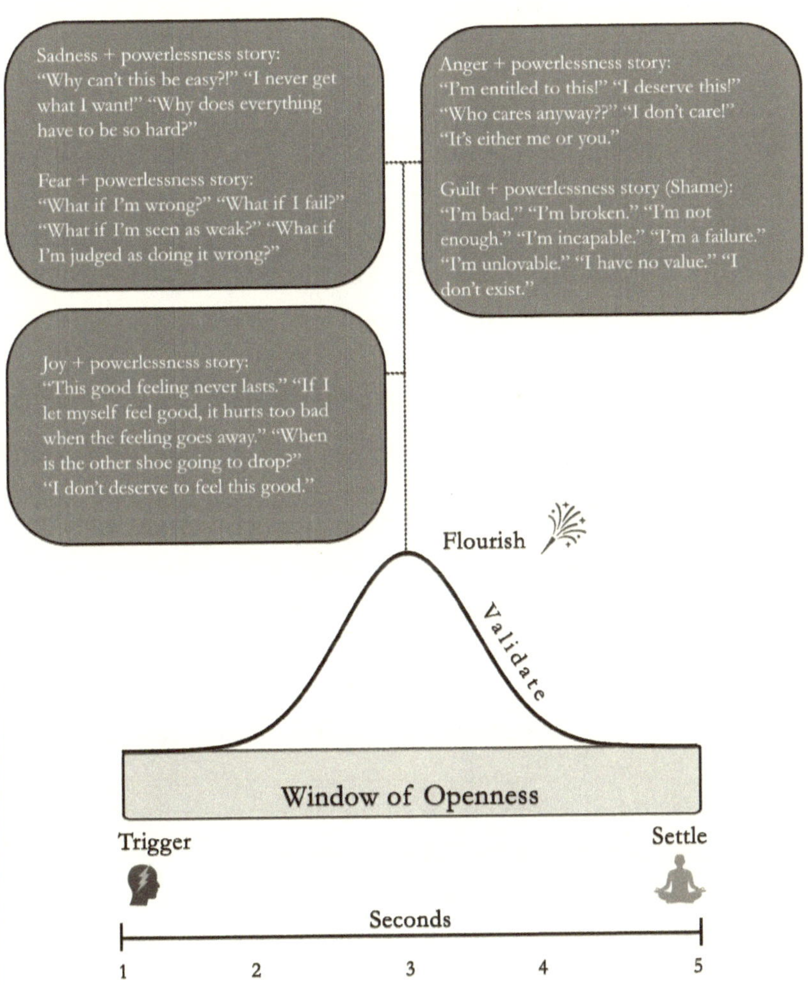

When we don't validate our needs and feelings, they turn into powerlessness stories we believe, and we get stuck in the flourish of feelings and don't make it back to settled.

- *If I'm vulnerable, I'll be attacked.*
- *I'm not enough as I am.*
- *I can't get my needs met unless I perform.*

These beliefs aren't true, but they feel true when they hijack our mind and body. They shape our actions and perceptions.

The Express Lane graphic shows the difference between feeling our feelings from power (perceiving no threat to our worthiness) and feeling our feelings from powerlessness (Oh yeah—there's something wrong with me).

Many of us have been trained to have our feelings immediately drop us into powerless. This training can be transformed by validating the unmet need that is activating the powerlessness.

- *Validation*: Yes, we were trained to believe that the only way to regulate our uncomfortable feelings is by trying to prevent them from happening.
- *Simple Truth*: We learned to try to control the external world and the people in it so our fears about ourselves wouldn't come up.
- *Validating Truth*: The truth about us is that we can regulate our feelings by validating them. More about this very soon. The use of *we* and *us* validates both the present-moment you and the past versions of you who lived the experience.

When these beliefs run the show, our prefrontal cortex shuts down. That's the part of our brain that can comfort and soothe us during our current experience so we are settled, present, and balanced. If no prefrontal cortex is online, we disconnect from our Essence and feel powerless to change.

Powerlessness dysregulates us. We try to escape by thinking our way out with defensive strategies. But the real path forward is to feel our way back in.

For example, believing *I'm not enough* might lead to procrastination, which is a defense against feeling guilt or shame. Dopamine, our

The Feelings "Express Lane" into Powerlessness

Healthy Feelings
Adaptive Action. *Body Sensations.*

Powerlessness Feelings
Body Sensations. Belief.

Healthy Feelings	Powerlessness Feelings
Sadness The loss of something wanted. *Releasing in throat, chest, and eyes.*	**Sadness + Powerlessness** *Extreme heaviness in chest, throat, and eyes.* I can't. I'm broken. I'm incapable. I did something wrong.
Fear Hey, look around. You're missing something. *Churning gut. Tightness in the belly.*	**Fear + Powerlessness** *Emptiness and tightness in the gut.* Why does this always happen to me? It's always going to be like this! Why can't this be easy?
Anger Teaching someone how to treat you. *Heat in the spine, upper back, and jaw.*	**Anger + Powerlessness** *Extreme heat rushing up the spine.* You made me wrong! Why do I always have to be the wrong one? You need to pay!
Guilt Self-reflection on whether your behavior was in integrity. *Collapsed energy in the body. Gut twisting.*	**Guilt + Powerlessness** *Extreme collapsing energy in the head and body, shame.* I'm wrong. I'm bad for what I did. The real me is unlovable. I'm bad for what I want.
Joy Motivated enthusiasm. *Exhilarating effervescence in the torso.*	**Joy + Powerlessness** *Openness and lightness into tightness and stuck energy.* Good feelings always go away. It won't last. Here are all of the reasons why I don't deserve to feel good.

motivation chemical, is MIA. When in Essence, we can validate the feeling and transform it from stuck energy and stuck beliefs into flowing energy and truth. Validations release dopamine in our brain. Dopamine helps us follow through. Creativity flows.

Self-Reflection

Essence cultivates self-reflection: the ability to pause and notice our inner state. Are we creating from curiosity or reacting from fear?

Self-reflection brings us back into learning mode. It opens the door to change. People who self-reflect feel safe to be around because they're settled.

What blocks self-reflection? Defensive mode. Strategies like hypervigilance, worry, and overanalysis masquerade as reflection but serve to avoid change.

In every moment, we have a choice: We can notice our state, validate our feelings, and choose responses other than reactive defensive strategies. We can remember what we want and find Essence-based ways to create it. We'll cover the steps to Validation soon.

My favorite way to generate self-reflection is from a both/and approach. For example, ask yourself how you are currently an extraordinary match as a partner, *and then* ask yourself how you're not an extraordinary match for someone. Asking for both perspectives opens your perception to seeing them both. Your defensive strategies will show you only one or a very limited perspective. Their job is to show you how you are or were the right one, so you're only looking for the right perspective that you alone have. Once you discover the ways you're not showing up in your extraordinary self, make a commitment to transform these patterns.

Simple Truth: Speaking Simple Truths and Validations to ourselves regulates our nervous system and transforms us from powerless to powerful.

Victim Powerlessness Perception

Powerlessness collapses our perception. We see only either/or outcomes. We feel like victims and look for villains. Our minds and our social media feed us fear-based narratives that seem true.

Examples of shifting from powerlessness to power

"Love is hard to find." → We attract love through self-love.
"I'm being rejected." → Our sense of self is un-rejectable.
"You're my enemy." → Let's cooperate to get both our needs met.

Check out the Victim Powerlessness graphics to understand more deeply how dangerous Victim powerlessness perception is to our ability to creatively problem-solve.

Many of the 60,000 thoughts we think each day are mediated by our powerlessness perception and the defensive thought strategies we deploy to get our power back. What we miss out on when we're consumed by this mind/body stuck and Stacked state is our creative mind, the part of us that can come up with solutions that work for everybody. Nothing new happens in victim powerlessness perception. Our perception is stuck and limited to one dimension: *I'm right! Someone has wronged me!* And most of the time, we don't know it, though others can see it. Our Pleaser strategies are futilely running around trying to get others' powerlessness to see things from a different perspective, right in the moment they can't. This causes a lot of unnecessary drama.

Victim Powerlessness Perception
Able to See That Transformation Is Possible

In an Essence-based state, the body feels safe and grounded, and the nervous system is regulated. Perception expands, allowing access to inner wisdom, empathy, and creative possibilities. Safety comes from within, making space for connection, choice, and real transformation.

Nervous System Shifts into Essence
- Calm, alert, socially engaged, breathing is deep and full.
- Feeling present, effervescent, and safe in our body.

Cognitive + Emotional
- Both/and thinking instead of either/or.
- Seeing the truth as layered, not binary.
- Able to see how things could change.
- Connecting with compassion.
- Value our experience and others without judgment.
- Creating what we want.

Body Sensations
- Muscles are relaxed.
- Posture is energized, grounded, and supported from within.
- Heartbeat is steady and calm.
- Feeling *in* our body vs. checked out.
- Vision is softer, more panoramic.
- A feeling of space and flow in the breath and body.

Perceptual Effects
- Ability to see with clarity, compassion, empathy, and engaged perception.
- Able to access moment-to-moment creativity and our innate value so ideas and spontaneity are popping.
- We see the inherent value of others.

Victim Powerlessness Perception
Unable to See That Transformation Is Possible

When our body is in a victim powerlessness state, it narrows what our mind can perceive. Although it's trying to keep us safe, this protective state actually blocks access to our deeper wisdom, authentic connection, and the possibility for real transformation.

Nervous System Shifts into Victim Powerlessness
- Autonomic nervous system moves into defensive protection mode.
- Body either braces for conflict or checks out entirely.

Cognitive + Emotional
- Safety over clairty is prioritized.
- Truth gets distorted.
- Uses right-or-wrong system as the truth.
- High functions like empathy, reflections, and problem-solving are less accessible.
- Seeing the world through a narrow lens that is focused on survival, threat, or blame.

Physical Symptoms
- Tightness in the chest, shoulders, jaw, or gut.
- Shallow or held breath.
- Heaviness, fatigue, or numbness.
- Racing thoughts or mental fog.
- Restlessness or shutdown.
- Emptiness.
- Draining energy.

Perceptual Effects
- Loss of access to Essence qualities like trust, creativity, and grounded presence.
- We see only limitations, problems, or danger. Belief that value is earned.
- Complaining, venting, or ruminating hijacks perception out of creative solutions.

Take a Moment to Choose This Moment

Start noticing when your thoughts or words drain you—
and when they empower you. Track your powerlessness
beliefs. Connect them to early experiences. Understanding their origin helps dissolve their hold.

Victim powerlessness perception makes us dangerously justifying beings. We justify our behavior based on what was done to us instead of acting from our core values. All wars, suicides, and the slow eroding of a great love are caused by Victim powerlessness perception. The eroding of great love alone can be an important motivator for you to learn everything you can about your past-down Victim powerlessness perception. See that play on words there? *Past* instead of *passed*. (Giggle.) Transforming this aspect of you is one of your life purposes because it is the biggest roadblock to who you really are.

The more you reconnect with Essence, the more you change your inner world and your life.

Welcome to the practice of returning to yourself.

We're learning about a lot of important and often unconsidered aspects of ourselves that are going on inside, right under our noses, such as Essence mode, defensive mode, Stacked body states, powerlessness beliefs and perception, and the sensations that signal them. These are all experiential systems that were trained to function through fear or Essence. It's very important to realize how many different experiential systems inside can be unconsciously trained to be dysfunctional and dysregulated. Let's learn about the observing awareness of these experiential systems as the first step to transforming any fear-based systems back into Essence.

CHAPTER 2

Transform Your Unconscious Procedural Manual

"I didn't fall in love; I rose in it."

—Toni Morrison

Previously, we explored the foundational idea that your inner world can be consciously navigated. That you can transform non-Essencey parts of you back into Essence. Now let's deepen awareness by building the skill you'll need, learning how to compassionately observe the body's energy and reactions so they can transform.

My mother often complained about my father and believed he needed to change. And to be fair, he did. But the way she went about trying to initiate that change was deeply flawed. She was unconsciously condescending, and her tone made him feel wrong for being stuck in his patterns. Her rightness triggered his wrongness, and they'd fall into familiar bickering matches that escalated into arguments, followed by days of stonewalling. This dynamic became the backdrop of my childhood.

I took after my father in many ways, so eventually my mother began treating me the same way. She had valid needs like wanting consistency and reliability, but the way she tried to meet those needs backfired. She unintentionally reenacted a despairing cycle where her needs went unmet, and she passed that pattern on to me. Through what I call the Unconscious Procedural Manual, she handed me a double bind: the belief that others didn't care about my needs and the defensive strategy of making others wrong when my needs weren't met. Great relationship training, right?

For two decades, I consciously avoided replicating my parents' harsh words. I didn't attack anyone's character. But what I didn't realize was that my tone—my condescension and resentments—still caused harm. My unconscious was expressing what I was trying so hard not to say out loud.

Life on Autopilot

Your conscious mind can only hold so much information at once. Beneath that awareness is your unconscious, which runs all your automatic processes like walking, brushing your teeth, driving familiar routes, and even making that satisfied *aah* after you drink water. Automatic actions like these, stemming from what is known technically as implicit memory, form your Unconscious Procedural Manual. This system governs 95 percent of your daily behaviors, using memories of the past to solve current problems. This would be a great system if we were all taught to be in our Essence all the time. It filters out what's deemed unimportant and brings our attention to what feels essential to survival, particularly threats to our sense of self.

How was this manual programmed? It began in infancy, based on how your caregivers responded to their own unmet needs. My unconscious manual, for example, was trained to respond with fighty anger when I feel unheard. Fighty anger needs someone to be wrong. Consciously, I know anger doesn't help me be heard, but years of witnessing fighty anger taught my brain and body to use it anyway.

Your manual carries beliefs about how lovable, powerful, safe, and valuable you are. It stores your earliest perceptions of self-worth, all shaped by your caregivers and how they dealt with emotions. If your father felt unappreciated and ranted about "entitled people," you might have learned to stay quiet, have few needs, and avoid becoming one of those "stupid people." If your mother shut down her feelings, and so didn't know how to help you with yours, your Unconscious Procedural Manual might be imprinted with "My feelings don't matter."

When you feel powerless, your manual activates inherited defensive strategies. As much as we may dislike the patterns we learned from our caregivers, they live on in us until we transform them. Exploring how you got or didn't get your needs met as a child is the first step in transforming these unconscious procedures.

We begin developing our sense of self in infancy. Babies are deeply connected to their Essence, and spending time with a baby naturally draws out our own Essence. When caregivers meet children from their Essence, it reinforces the child's connection to their own. But if parents meet children from their defenses, the child's sense of self becomes entangled with powerlessness and inherited defensive strategies.

For example, if you were labeled "shy" as a child, you might have internalized a belief that you're socially awkward and safer alone. But what if your fears had been validated, your courage reflected back to you? You might have developed social confidence instead.

According to developmental psychologist Allan Schore, infants' sense of self is shaped in the first eighteen months of life through right-brain maturation. This period is when the Unconscious Procedural Manual is formed. It may not be remembered with words, but it's deeply stored in the body.

So, what helps a child develop a self-image connected to Essence rather than fear and defense? Validation. When parents validate their child's emotions while remaining in their own Essence, the child learns to self-regulate and stay connected to their truth. Validate to regulate.

From the graphic on the following page we can see how the Unconscious Procedural Manual gets its training in fear and defenses. No one wants this to happen. It happens because there is a lot in our Unconscious Procedural Manual that we aren't aware of until we teach ourselves to become aware of it. Your awareness level has a huge impact on those around you.

When caregivers express fighty anger such as blame, fault-finding, or the need to be right, they disconnect from both their own Essence and their child's. The child perceives this withdrawing of Essencey energy as everything good being withdrawn from them because their sense of self is bad. The caretaker is shrinking their Essence energy into contracted defensive strategies. The child misinterprets this as saying something about *them*. Authentic anger, by contrast, maintains connection to Essence while setting boundaries respectfully.

Imagine a child crying over a lost stuffed animal. A parent in defensive mode might rush them or get angry. A parent in Essence validates both their own stress (*We're scared we're going to be late!*) and the child's pain (*You miss your stuffy*), modeling emotional regulation and equally valid experiences for both the parent and the child. When we could feel our caregivers trying to understand our experience, our experience transformed. When we felt them "shoulding" our experience, as in, (*you shouldn't be feeling that way*), our experience got stuck in the feeling as we tried harder to get them to validate it.

Unfortunately, many parents punish children for emotional expressions they themselves trained into them. Children reflect what they observe. If you want to know how you or your partner handles frustration, look at your child's reactions to frustration.

How Unconscious Processes Are Passed Down

ESSENCE

When the parent meets the child's Essence with Essence, the child imprints the self as Essence and the observing awareness behind the Essence.

Free-flowing energy. No sense-of-self threat

STACK

When the parent meets the child's Essence from defensive strategies, the child begins to feel powerless. Their Essence is not enough, lovable, worthy, capable, or safe.

Contracted energy. Threatened sense of self.

STACK

In order to be who their parent's defensive strategies need the child to be, the child steps out of their Essence and into their learned Pleaser defensive strategies.

We now know infants as young as two months can detect whether their caregiver is in Essence or defense. Infants try to keep their caregivers in their Essence by learning to avoid behaviors that seem to send the parent into their defenses. This is people pleaser training instead of Essence training. These patterns get embedded long before most of us even realize.

Take a Moment to Choose This Moment

Reflect on your developing sense of self. What did you learn as a child about how to relate to your internal world? Were you taught to regulate your emotions with Essence or defenses? Did you see your caregivers pause and reflect during conflict? Was your internal experience validated? Were you taught how body states influence perception? If your answer is no, you're not alone. Let's leave defensive blame in the rearview and focus on attuning inward. Your caregivers didn't teach you because they weren't taught either. Their defensive strategies hijacked their ability to validate your experience.

Your sense of self was imprinted with a lot of powerlessness beliefs about feelings, needs, your body, and how to relate to yourself and others. You're learning to transform your sense of self back into authentic power instead of the pseudo-power of defensive strategies by validating your training as distinct from the truth about you. You're also learning how to discern whether someone is in Essence or defensive strategies as the way to know whether they are speaking truth. This allows you to remain calm and collected when others are on autopilot in defensive strategies.

Brain Wiring and Mirror Neurons

One key takeaway is that unconscious patterns are passed down through mirror neurons, brain cells that activate both when we perform an action and when we observe someone else performing it. They help us "mirror" others internally.

According to Dan Siegel, our mirror neurons wire us to match the emotional patterns of significant people in our lives. When we were infants, we mapped our parents' behaviors. If they shut down when fearful, so did we. If they exploded in anger, we learned to do the same. If they were hardwired to only be able to focus on their experience, we have that strategy. If they got stuck in powerlessness for days on end, we're going to have those days.

Our neural networks are full of these inherited patterns. Sometimes, we're not even reacting from ourselves; we're mirroring unexamined strategies passed down across generations. One of my clients realized she had been passed down a system where activating the contractor muscles in the front of her body and deactivating the extensor muscles in the back of her body was the way to be in a body. This resulted in all kinds of pain because of the misalignment it caused. Once she validated this as a belief and spoke the truth about how her contractors and extensors could enjoy a balance, she came instantly back into alignment.

Observing Awareness

Your observing awareness is the part of you that watches thoughts, sensations, and feelings without being swept into them. It lives in the middle prefrontal cortex, the part of the brain responsible for empathy, self-regulation, and perspective.

The right prefrontal cortex nurtures and soothes. The left makes sense of sensations and experiences. When trauma-trained beliefs trigger painful thoughts (like *My feelings don't matter*), the right cortex shuts down, and defensive strategies kick in, obsessing, judging, numbing.

To reconnect to the truth about us, we need to validate to regulate. Validation regulates our emotions and our sense-of-self alert mode and our nervous system from the inside using internal actions.

Validate the belief: We were trained to feel unworthy because some emotional needs went unmet.

Notice the familiar pain showing up as body sensations when you express this Validation to yourself out loud.

The *We* in the previous Validation refers to your present self and the past versions of you that didn't get the need met.

Locate your sense of self as your observing awareness and not your body sensations. You can call back the Bicycle Wheel of Awareness mentioned in the introduction by envisioning your observing awareness in the hub and your body sensations of powerlessness and unmet needs on the rim. From the safety of the hub, you're validating the momentary experiences happening out on the rim so they can transform from rigid and pressurized either/ors back into easy flowing both/ands. (We will continue to learn more about either/ors and both/ands throughout the book.)

It can be startling how much of our lives we've been trained to spend out on the rim of the Bicycle Wheel of Awareness (see graphic on next page). Look at all the time we've spent fused with our thoughts, feelings, or defensive strategies. The rim is chaotic and overwhelming and a constant source of threat to our nervous system. If we are graceful and kind in the way that we look at this, though, it makes a lot more sense why many of us have trouble feeling satisfied and fulfilled with our lives and opens us to the hope and the pathway to find our fulfillment. If there are two different versions of us, trained-in fear (rim) and Essence (hub), we can transform the rim by relearning to trust our hub-y Essence.

The spokes on this Bicycle Wheel of Awareness represent either threats to the sense of self (unworthiness of getting a need met) that push us out to the rim, or the Essence qualities that carry us back to the hub.

Bicycle Wheel of Awareness

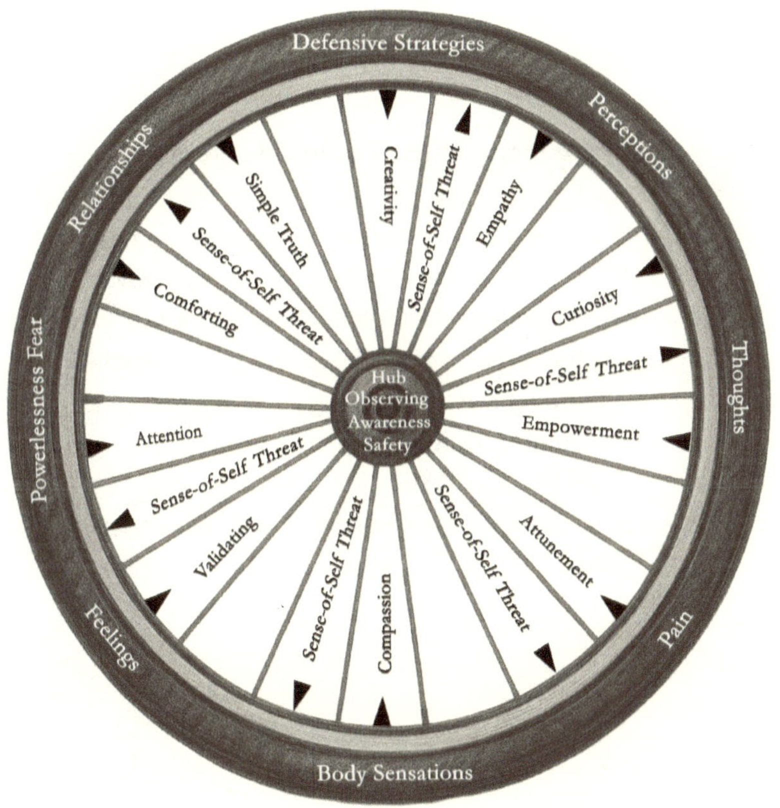

When the sense of self is located in the hub of the wheel, experiences are perceived as manageable. When the sense of self spins out to the rim, experiences feel unsafe, overwhelming, and out of control.

Adapted from Dan Siegel's "Wheel of Awareness" 2018

Validations activate the ventral vagal nerve, which calms the body and reconnects us to Essence. Notice on the Bicycle Wheel of Awareness how Essence qualities, like Validations, Simple Truth, curiosity, and compassion, transform the fears about our sense of self so we can reside in the hub. Experiencing transformation this way allows us to trust it and finally let go of trusting our defensive strategies. Who knew that fear simply needs soothing to transform?!

Take a Moment to Choose This Moment

Can you locate a place of safety in your body—chest, gut, feet? Most of us weren't trained to feel safe inside. We were trained to try to control for our safety by managing how others see us. This inner anchor of safety within the body is where observing awareness resides. It's your internal lighthouse during storms. Speak a *Simple Truth* from this safety place: "I know we're scared we did something wrong. From this safe observing awareness inside, we can feel our connection to our inner strength while we're feeling some fear move through."

The graphic on the next page demonstrates how unmet needs imprint on our emotions and how we're susceptible to using defensive strategies to get them met instead of our caring Essence. This goes south so quickly for us that it scares us into believing that no one really cares about our needs.

We've been learning about how our sense of self has an Unconscious Procedural Manual it sources itself from. This manual was passed down through mirror neurons to have both Essence and

Your Caring Nature
in Order to Get Needs Met

When in Essence

When on a Stack

Authentic care for others invites the same in return.

Needs are met with ease, creating a sense of empowerment.

The person believes their needs can be met and feels free to co-create meaningful connection with others to get all needs met.

Using defensive strategies often triggers that in others.

This creates a cycle where no one feels heard or understood.

The person ends up feeling powerless believing no one really cares about their needs.

They lash out in anger or fall into despair.

- Consciously and unconsciously creates harmony.
- Capable of being caring while getting needs met.

- Consciously wants harmony.
- Unconsciously inflicts harm.
- Uncaring for others while trying to get needs met.

powerlessness fear programmed into it about how much love, power, value, and safety we are worthy of. We're also discovering how we can identify the sense of self as the observing awareness, which can step back outside the experience to be the noticing validator of it. This gives us the perspective we need, to know that we aren't the experience we're having. We are the observer of it. As the observer of it, we can have influence on it. We can transform our inner experience.

CHAPTER 3

Defensive Strategies

Previously, we began tuning into body-based awareness. We explored how to take the internal actions of
becoming your observing awareness and validating
your current experience to transform some unhelpful and
untrue training. (More about this soon.) Now we'll explore how your nervous system can misfire into defensive
strategies that block connection with your Essence.

Integrating the Concept by Having the Experience

Let's say I introduce a concept like this: Either/ors can limit experiential learning, while both/ands can expand it. How do we move that
from a concept into an embodied experience? Conceptual learning

allows us to categorize information. It is how we learn the steps and know what to do. Experiential learning, however, integrates new information through the body. It wires that learning into the Unconscious Procedural Manual so it can run automatically in the future. You can tell when Essence is integrated into your Unconscious Procedural Manual by noticing: 1) Less anger and defensiveness in your response to challenges, 2) more flexibility and creativity in how you perceive what's happening, and 3) a body-felt empowerment of your power to transform unwanted experiences.

The key is not to decide which type of learning is "better." Both conceptual and experiential learning have value. When we bring awareness to how and when we use each, we gain internal balance. In that regulated state, we can access our inherent wisdom and transform concepts into genuine realization.

In *The Let Them Theory*, Mel Robbins says we can use comparisons like either/ors to either teach or torture depending on how we use them. For example, using the comparison of Essence or fear, we can make fear the wrong experience and torture ourselves when in it, or we can learn from the comparison about the different results we get with each. If comparisons are used to learn from both sides of the polarity, they are Essencey. If used to make one side better than the other, they are defensive.

Simple Truth: Both/ands create new experiences; defensive either/ors cause experiences to get stuck on repeat.

Have you ever noticed how when someone comes at you with a "this or that" argument, your own system automatically reacts with its own version of either/or? You either appease or oppose. You either speak up or shut down. When we're in a polarized mindset of either/or, neither party can be in the internal state necessary for mutual understanding, (both/and).

Why do we do this? Because our Unconscious Procedural Manual perceives threats from either/ors and relaxes into both/ands. Either/ors pressure us into one end of polarity while both/ands allow us to meet in the middle.

If we encounter a new concept that conflicts with our unconscious programming and we don't transform the experience in our Unconscious Procedural Manual, the concept won't hold. We'll end up disappointed, feeling like nothing works.

So, how do we bridge that gap?

Think of your left brain as loving concepts; that's its jelly. It wants to make sense of things. Your right brain loves experience; that's its peanut butter. When your left brain helps make sense of your right brain's rich connection to your body, you create a whole sandwich of concept and experience together. This is embodiment. You not only know what's true, but you also feel it inside you.

Trauma disrupts this flow. Trauma is anything that pulls you out of Essence and into a powerlessness state. Many of our traumas stem from being met with our caregivers' either/or defensive strategies. Our caregivers unintentionally trained our nervous systems to search for external right-or-wrong threats instead of relying on internal truth.

Your Experiential Systems Need Your Attention

Let's understand this from a both/and perspective. Instead of pitting ideas against each other, we look at the value each offers. There are multiple experiential systems inside us that guide how we feel, decide, and relate:

- Emotional system: feelings
- Sense-of-self system: where we source from
- Attentional system: where we focus
- Inner truth system: relaxed, open awareness
- Pain system: response to internal discomfort
- Reward system: how we savor or celebrate Essence
- Right or wrong system: trained-in shoulds
- Appraisal system: how we assign meaning

These systems influence our physical ones (muscular, cardiovascular, respiratory, nervous, etc.). Fear felt in the emotional system can hijack all other systems, disconnecting us from Essence.

The sense-of-self system is the one most disrupted. This is where we source our inner truth. When trauma wires fear into this system, we armor ourselves in defensive mode. That armor skews our perceptions, reactions, and beliefs.

Here's how it plays out:

- Emotional system: overwhelmed by fear
- Attentional system: narrowed to fear-based either/or thinking
- Inner truth: inaccessible
- Appraisal system: high alert for threats of wrongness
- Pain system: activated into powerlessness
- Reward system: internal dopamine offline/seeking external dopamine of being right
- Right or wrong: rigidly active

This cascade affects our physical systems too: tense muscles, shallow breathing, increased heart rate. Our sense of self fuses with fear. Imagine what this does to our bodies over time.

We're learning a lot about important aspects of ourselves going on inside. A lot of experiential systems that were trained to function through fear or Essence, requiring our physical systems to function from fear or Essence. It's very important to realize how our experiential systems can be trained in dysfunction and dysregulation. Learning to be the observing awareness of these experiential systems inside is what allows us to begin to transform any systems from fear back into Essence. If you transform the experiential systems, you automatically transform your physical systems. You can have a huge impact on how your physical body functions by doing this internal transformation.

Confusion Fusion of the Sense of Self

You may have never thought about how you sense your self internally before reading this book. Our sense of self can fuse with any internal experiential system. One minute you're calm and grounded; the next, you've become your inner critic or people-pleaser. Understanding where your sense of self is in any moment makes conscious choice possible.

Think of your sense of self like a basketball. Your sense-of-self ball bouncing between players (different systems). One team is Essence; the other is defensive strategies. The sense of self bouncing around inside can be very confusing until you become aware of it.

Example: I was biking and had to veer slightly to avoid a puddle. I was proactive and signaled the cars about my maneuver. A car honked anyway, and my sense-of-self system instantly fused with my childhood belief: *I'm being blamed no matter how hard I try.* My appraisal system triggered fighty anger: *Can't you see what I'm up against here? Have a heart!* (yes, with exaggerated hand gestures and all).

Later, I got curious about my reaction and giggled, realizing the honk was short, not long, and had likely just been a friendly hello. But fused with my past pain, my sense-of-self system had perceived blame and reacted from an old wound. Someone wanted to say hi. I accused them of heartlessness. Misinterpret much?

When you understand this fusion process, past confusing behavior makes sense. Familiar stuck beliefs show up in your thoughts, familiar stuck feelings in your body. These are patterned signs your sense of self is fused with fear. Which leads to defensiveness. Then to reacting to what you don't want instead of creating what you do from Essence.

Our sense of self can fuse with our body sensations and our feelings, and when this happens, both become overwhelming. Of course we're overwhelmed! Our sense of self just got hijacked right smack into the middle of the body's experiences. When you learn the skill of validating the feelings and body sensations, you become fused with the observing awareness that can transform them from the outside.

Yes, your defensive strategies also get fused with your sense of self: Punisher, People-pleaser, Protector. Many of us are exhausted at the end of the day simply because we've been fused with our people-pleaser all day. One moment you're in Essence, creating; the next you're reacting, then justifying or judging your reaction.

Our sense of self can bounce around inside, melding with different aspects of us in there and yet still maintain a consistent sense of self. There's a lot that has been going on in there that has been running under our conscious radar.

Simple Truth: Someone else's defensive mode says nothing about our worth and a lot about their fears. Notice how your body responds.

Simple Truth: When we make sense of our behavior through experiential learning (noticing how our body responds), we can transform our powerlessness and defensive strategies back into Essence. Notice how your body responds.

Take a Moment to Choose This Moment

Reflect on a time when you were swept into a Stacked automatic reaction. See if you can look through the lens of your compassionate observing awareness. How did your sense of self bounce around, fusing with your body sensations? With your thoughts? With your powerlessness? With your defensive strategies? Notice how your fears and defensive strategies knock you away from your core values (your Essence).

Be compassionate with yourself. These parts have worked hard to try to regulate your feelings and meet unmet needs, even if they've caused chaos along the way. Appreciate your defensive strategies so

The Fusion of the Sense of Self

**POWERLESSNESS FEAR
experienced as:**

Defensiveness,
fear or anticipation
of threat

A reactor on
autopilot

Fusing with the
body sensations
of tightness and
pain

**ESSENCE
experienced as:**

Openness, trust,
and inner safety

Sudden inspiration
and delight in creativity

Embodied inner
calm, presence,
and harmony

they can relinquish their extremes and relax back into trusting the Essence within them. We're not leaving anyone behind.

Essence Breathing

Our respiratory system often responds to fear with shallow, tight breathing. Essence breathing is free, flowing, and calming. It tells your body: *You are safe.* It allows you to create safety within when you would normally get stuck in perceiving threats. Essence breathing is a way your experiential systems can have an Essencey impact on your physical systems.

The sense-of-self threat alert system (the autonomic nervous system) has a few branches. The sympathetic branch revs us up from powerlessness fear or the excitement and enthusiasm from Essence. And the parasympathetic branch comforts and soothes our fears when we're in Essence or shuts us down emotionally when we're in fear and defensive mode.

Trauma from our caretakers' defensive strategies gets embodied as chronic fear-based sympathetic nervous system activation without the parasympathetic nervous system's Essencey vagal brake. The parasympathetic brake is activated by Essence breathing.

Three steps to Essence breathing

1. Inhale deeply until it feels like your breath reaches your pelvic floor (even though it physiologically can't).
2. Exhale slowly, slightly longer than usual.
3. As you exhale, notice your body letting go.

Your pelvic floor often holds tension from physical and emotional trauma. Most people don't realize how tight it is until they start relaxing it. When it loosens, fear may surface because the tightness was trying to protect you by trapping the fear in it. Meet those sensations with Essence: *I'm learning to be with fear, not afraid of it.*

Essence breathing rewires your Unconscious Procedural Manual about how to feel safe in your body. Noticing your breath daily helps you regulate your body's sense of safety. If you notice you're breathing shallowly, you're on alert and not feeling safe. You can practice Essence breathing and bring yourself back into an internally safe mode each time you go on alert until your body's default mode is Essence breathing.

Take a Moment to Choose This Moment

Contemplate what healing means. It's not perfection—it's transformation through new experiences. When you bring warmth and presence to parts of you trained in fear, you meet a previously unmet need. And in doing so, the psychological wound begins to heal, to transform.

Window of Openness

HYPERAROUSAL

Identifies with Defensive Strategies

You feel extremely reactive, angry, manic, or out of control due to a perceived threat to your sense of self. Mind races, and inner body contracts into either/or thinking that seems helpful but causes chaos.

REVVING UP DYSREGULATION

Identifies with Defensive Strategies

You feel agitated, anxious, revved up, or angry due to a perceived threat to your sense of self. Mind closes. Body tightens. Misperceiving reality into either/ors.

WINDOW OF OPENNESS

Identifies with Essence

You are open to learning, especially about yourself. Your mind is open. Your body is in ease and flow. You are in presence and in the moment. You are creating new both/and experiences in each moment.

SHUTTING DOWN DYSREGULATION

Identifies with Powerlessness

You feel low energy, confused, shut down, or sinking due to perceived threats to your sense of self. Your mind becomes disoriented, shutting off from your body, and distorts reality into either/ors.

HYPOAROUSAL

Identifies with Powerlessness

Your energy is extremely immobilized. Your mind zones out and your body numbs out due to a perceived threat to self. Your mind can't imagine itself outside of powerlessness, so your body's light dims away.

Adapted from Dr. Dan Siegel, MD "Window of Tolerance"

The Window of Openness

Your window of openness, also referred to by Stephen Porges as the social engagement system, is your physiological state when no threat is perceived. It's the state in which you can connect deeply to yourself and others.

Adapted from Dan Siegel's "window of tolerance," the Window of Openness graphic shows how nervous system states affect perception, learning, and you just being you. In alert mode (dysregulation, hyper/hypo), we can't learn or change. Our physiology is locked into old beliefs and fear.

The hyper/hypo zones are intense enough that we know we're in them. The revved-up and shut-down dysregulation zones are the tricky ones. We're functional in these dysregulation zones, but we're still perceiving threats to our sense of self, so we're functioning from defensive strategies and not Essence. Many of us, in how we sense our selves internally, were trained to live in this dysregulation zone almost all the time.

Our Pleasers reside in the dysregulation zone. Not knowing how to be in the present moment of the window of openness, they vigilantly toil away, reenacting our past fears into an inflexible future. They are trying to be loved and valued for being what others need them to be instead of listening to their inner truth.

Our Protectors also reside in the dysregulation zone. They are so busy trying to control us, others, and events that they wear us out with all the things that could go wrong. They are vigilantly yoked to the belief that if they focus on what could go wrong, they can make it right.

Our Punishers reside in the dysregulation zone too. They are so focused on us not being let down or disappointed again. They are vigilant about setting the whole thing right. The way they go about it, though, activates others to go on alert and resist or acquiesce, so Punishers get our needs met through force and not genuine equality.

In threat mode, we can't perceive reality clearly. Everything feels like an attack, a trap, or a power play. It feels like something is being

How Our Nervous System Distorts the Truth

SYMPATHETIC HYPERAROUSAL
High Stress Alert

- Reality is seen through extreme right or wrong thinking, fueling hate or destruction toward self and others.
- Energy feels out of control, pushing into Pleaser, Protector, or Punisher modes.
- Truth feels threatening, so only validation of victimhood is accepted.
- Thinking becomes either/or, leading to actions that seem dramatic or overblown to others.
- Aggression feels like the only way to survive; rage can be triggered by a sense of being stopped, blocked, or annihilated.

SYMPATHETIC REVVING UP DYSREGULATION
Elevated Alert

- Driven by old powerlessness beliefs but interpreted as threats from the outside.
- Defensive strategies replace Essence qualities.
- Opinions and knowledge are mistaken for the self.
- Care or comfort feels invalidating.
- Reactions are hijacked by the past; meanings come from old experiences.
- Behavior is justified with "I am the Victim!" and stories that reinforce that identity.
- Truth feels like a personal attack and is rejected to protect the sense-of-self.

SOCIAL ENGAGEMENT
Window of Openness

- The body and emotions are calm, and reality is clear.
- No threats are perceived to the sense-of-self.
- Access to abundant Essence qualities and internal resources.
- Perceptions are grounded in truth rather than right or wrong thinking.
- Can see others' defensive strategies without taking them personally.
- Experience self as capable and creative.
- Attention is conscious, with awareness valuing internal experience.

PARASYMPATHETIC SHUTTING DOWN DYSREGULATION
Shut Down Alert

- Reality is filtered through powerlessness, making the self feel under threat.
- Defensive strategies (avoiding, withdrawing, self-blaming, dissociating) replace Essence.
- Perceptions are either/or and tied to Pleaser, Protector, or Punisher thinking.
- The self feels blocked by forces beyond its control.

PARASYMPATHETIC RED ZONE
Deep Shut Down

- Reality feels hopeless and meaningless; nothing matters.
- Body feels heavy, numb, tight, or sick; shame and darkness dominate.
- The self feels erased or hijacked by past powerlessness pain.
- No motivation to change; suicidal thoughts or actions can arise from this state.
- Feels like the self will be destroyed if it tries to be authentic.

done to us that is keeping us from thriving. That's the Unconscious Procedural Manual running the show. The following graphic displays how our Unconscious Procedural Manual can function under our awareness, distorting our perception in the name of fighting against our own past pain in the present moment.

The chart on the previous page shows how our thoughts, perceptions, and therefore, feelings change depending on which zone we're in within the window of openness.

We confuse psychological fears with real life-and-limb danger. Our bodies respond to internal stories as if they're real. Until we shine loving awareness on these patterns, we stay stuck on a hamster wheel of unmet needs and defensive habits.

The window of openness graphic can help you visualize where your sense of self is located. You want to increase your skills of sensing these internal state changes. Using this visual you can remind yourself not to trust the way you're seeing yourself or the world when you're dysregulated. Your powerlessness fears cloud your perception unless you're in the window of openness.

Some common sense-of-self threats (and the defensive strategies that mask them)—these may not feel like fear, but they're driven by powerlessness fear:

- Ruminating over how someone might have misread you (doing it wrong)
- Rigidly controlling choices or not choosing (creating chaos) to get your needs met (distrusting your inherent power)
- Repeating stories to prove your value (not having value)
- Dismissing or denying feedback (fear of vulnerability)
- Interrupting to assert your point (not trusting the self)
- Going silent to stay "safe" (not trusting expressing)
- Taking things personally (shame)
- Complaining or gossiping (not being good enough)

- Bragging or overpromoting (inferiority)
- Valuing intellect over emotion to avoid discomfort (fear of feeling out of control)
- Listening with a right or wrong filter (fear of being fundamentally flawed)

These examples have been simplified for easy understanding and to inspire more exploration on your part. Suggestion alert (it's just a suggestion—you don't have to take it): Consider talking to a trusted other or a developmental trauma or body-centered therapist to go deeper and feel supported in new ways.

Take a Moment to Choose This Moment

Reflect: What sense-of-self threats do you identify with from the list above? Which defensive strategies? Explore who might have passed down these defensive strategies to you. They are not your creative spirit, so they were passed down from someone. Meet these fears and defensive strategies with curiosity and compassion so your learning can deepen, and your past pain can heal in the presence of Essence this time around. Try this: Picture yourself as a child of different ages. Speak directly to those past versions of you: "Hey, little ones, I see you. We're feeling the same pain. I know you need to be understood. You matter to me. I care about what you need." It might feel strange at first, but it's profoundly healing for the past versions of you to feel in the present moment that you validate them. Give yourself what you didn't get, and the need begins to feel worthy.

Every time your nervous system goes into alert mode, it reveals an unmet need. A regulated nervous system doesn't perceive threats to the self; it knows its needs are worthy. Unmet needs feel like threats to the self. Your defensive strategies have been trying to regulate your feelings by locating the threats to you through blame, judgments, and closed-mindedness. Let's appreciate their endless effort and validate the limited training they received about how to regulate the alert system, so they can learn new ways to regulate. Validate to regulate, baby!

Simple Truth: I appreciate the heck out of you, blaming and judging Protectors, for instilling a sense of rightness as power before we knew how to access our inner truth as power.

A Personal Story

As a child, I clung to my mom's leg in a store while she chatted with another mom. I played peekaboo with the baby in a nearby stroller. Suddenly, my mom yanked me away and yelled, "Don't make that baby's eyes move like that! You'll make it go blind!"

She never explained it. But I carried that terror for weeks, convinced we'd get a call at any moment saying the baby had indeed gone blind because of me.

It wasn't a one-time event. It patterned me with a core wound: *No matter what I do, I'm fundamentally wrong.* That belief lived in my nervous system, in my emotions, in my appraisal of the world.

Later in life, when someone tried to be "right," I fused with the belief that I was "wrong." My body collapsed into shame, my brain shut down, and I lost access to self-compassion.

I could still function, but my people-pleaser was in overdrive. I needed experiential learning, not more ideas but felt experiences that could rewire my system.

I finally began to understand what Michael Singer meant by the "roommate in our head," our observing awareness. The challenge wasn't the idea (I got that); it was integrating it into my body so I could use it in the moments I needed it. Validations meet the unmet need by giving the need value that it didn't receive before. Meet the need and the defensive strategies relax back into their more flexible authentic versions. They no longer need to prove the self is worthy; they just feel it internally. Validate to rewire.

> "Learning is the process whereby knowledge is
> created through the transformation of experience."
>
> —David A. Kolb

CHAPTER 4

Unmet Needs

List of Unmet Needs Covered in This Book

- The need to have our internal experience validated
- The need for mind/body connection
- The need for a sense of belonging
- The need for a regulated nervous system
- The need for an internal sense of agency and power
- The need to be comforted and soothed with Simple Truths
- The need to be taught about internal resources of abundance
- The need to be taught about the power of choice
- The need to have our Essence qualities appreciated as the way to create change
- The need to have our vulnerability transformed into authenticity
- The need for unconditional love from Essence

- The need to feel safe to be our Essence instead of people-pleasers
- The need to be taught how to receive by trying things on in our body
- The need to be taught to connect to our moment-to-moment creativity
- The need to be taught how to trust ourselves by connecting to our inner truth
- The need to be taught confidence to explore unknowns through our autonomy
- The need to connect with others for a sense of community

Previously, we explored defensive strategies—those well-practiced behaviors designed to protect us from internal discomfort. Now, we'll journey to the source of those strategies: unmet needs. These are the core emotional experiences we longed for but didn't consistently receive, and they are often still directing our lives from the shadows.

I've spent my whole life trying to be the chosen one, the one who was wanted. When I was young, my brother seemed to be the chosen one for my mother. He learned to stuff his feelings, just like she did, while I acted mine out, echoing my father. My mom criticized my father and tried to criticize my father out of me. The pain of not being wanted by my mom, as my inner systems interpreted it, was so unbearable I would have done anything to avoid feeling that shame. Being wanted became my deepest unmet need. Feeling powerless about being wanted became my most painful, shame-filled belief.

Since I couldn't win over my mom, I turned to my dad. He was a coach, so I figured if I could become great at sports, better than my brother, I could earn his love. That belief shaped my personality and taught me to try to get my needs met externally from others instead of internally from my own Essencey resources. I became a people-pleasing overachiever. I asked questions, listened attentively, and made others feel special so they felt wanted like I wanted to feel and so they'd want to be around me. When people liked me, I felt wanted. *So* external.

Of course, when I was alone, I fell apart. I didn't know who I was without bouncing my identity off someone else. I needed other people to meet my unsatisfiable need, and yet I interpreted so many of their actions as rejections. It was unsatisfiable because I felt a longing from unworthiness instead of worthiness. My unfulfilled need for being wanted/chosen caused so much shame it was overwhelming. I began bingeing and purging to distract myself from my feelings and numb out. I had no tools to transform what I was feeling. I had never been validated for my insides. I had no idea that what I truly needed was already within me, just waiting for my transforming attention.

At the time, I couldn't have told you the difference between Essence and fear. I had no concept of my internal landscape. Validation, schmalidation! Looking inside felt like walking into a haunted house. The real monsters, I thought, were in there.

Get to Know Your Unmet Needs

Now that you're familiar with your defensive strategies, it's time to explore more about where they come from: your unmet needs. These aren't minor preferences; they're fundamental emotional experiences that many of us didn't have growing up. Not because our parents were bad people, but because they themselves weren't trained to meet these needs. Their emotional needs weren't met either. Most of our families didn't have any idea how to regulate feelings by validating needs.

Most defensive strategies are external attempts to meet internal needs. But here's the paradox: Those very strategies often block us from receiving what we need. The solution isn't to try harder or look harder outside us—it's to turn our attention inward, with compassion. Bringing Essence qualities to meet unmet needs transforms them.

These needs may feel unfamiliar at first and yet oddly recognizable, like meeting a long-lost part of yourself.

A note on blame: When you begin to see what was missing, it's natural to want to blame the people who raised you. But blaming keeps you stuck in defensive mode. Even if someone were to blame, blame doesn't reconnect you to Essence. Compassion does. You can teach your inner blamer that validating your pain is more powerful than assigning fault.

Four Common Unmet Needs

My story was about the unmet need of feeling valued for my unique experience. There are so many emotional needs that went unmet even though most of my physical needs were taken care of. Let's explore four common unmet needs: mind/body connection, regulated nervous system, belonging, and personal power. We'll explore more unmet needs in the chapters that follow.

Mind/body connection

"The body is not a thing; it is a situation." —Jean-Paul Sartre

This unmet need is about having a loving, truth-based relationship between your mind and body. Most of us were trained to trust our minds and dismiss our bodies. But it's your body that sends you the earliest and truest signals about your internal state.

When you don't know how to connect your mind and body, your sense of self gets fused with powerlessness beliefs. These might sound like:

- *I am my thoughts.*
- *My body is unreliable or weak.*
- *If I feel this, I will fall apart and get stuck in it.*

To illustrate, I had a client whose partner was laid off. Immediately, her mind went into overdrive: catastrophic thoughts about the future, financial fears, and feelings of being unsupported. For herself, not her partner! She became irritable and shut down emotionally.

As we worked together, she realized that she wasn't afraid of the layoff; she was afraid of the emotional disconnect it created inside her. She didn't know how to self-soothe. In her family, no one validated difficult emotions. When she didn't get that coregulation as a child, her nervous system had no idea how to offer it to her or to anyone else.

When I gave her experience value, validated her unmet need for comfort when afraid, and guided her into gentle connection with her body, she started to feel safe inside. Her jaw softened, her shoulders dropped, and her breathing deepened. Later, she told me, "I was finally able to attune to my partner's pain, without making it about me."

That's the power of mind/body integration. The body's experience transforms quickly when the mind shines Essencey attention on the body.

Regulated nervous system

"The nervous system is the foundation of our felt experience of safety."
—Deb Dana

Most of us were not taught how to regulate our nervous systems from Essence. We were taught to regulate them from defensive strategies instead. A regulated nervous system is a need that went unmet in most of us.

Our nervous systems develop in response to our caregivers. When they were calm and regulated, we learned to be calm and regulated. If they were anxious, reactive, or shut down, we absorbed that too. Your nervous system was shaped before you had language to describe what was happening.

Our autonomic nervous system, our sense-of-self threat alert mode, is in our brain stem, not our cortex. It's running under our awareness. Most people don't know they are feeling powerlessness fear because of this.

This is also why you might feel out of control or overwhelmed in conflict, even when there's no real danger. Your body is reliving past moments of internal threat. Emotions are flowing and not being validated. Defensive mode kicks in, narrowing your perception and distorting your reality.

Recognizing these threat stress reactions allows you to pause and make new choices. Validating your feelings settles your nervous system alert mode. With practice, you learn that you're not your reactions; you are the awareness that can choose how to respond to your reactions.

Belonging

"There is no greater suffering than feeling alone and no greater joy than feeling seen." —Anonymous

Belonging is a deep internal experience not just of being around people but of feeling like you matter to them. When we don't get this need met in childhood, we often try to earn our belonging later in life by performing, pleasing, or hiding parts of ourselves.

We internalize beliefs like:

- *If I show who I really am, I'll be rejected.*
- *I have to be who others want me to be to be loved.*
- *I'm only worthy if I contribute something.*

True belonging begins when we connect with our Essence and offer ourselves unconditional welcome. From that place, we attract relationships where we feel seen, known, and valued—not for what we do, but for who we are.

Personal power

"Real power comes not from force, but from presence." —Eckhart Tolle

Your power is the ability to create a desired effect internally and externally. Your choices either empower you or disempower you. Your thoughts either empower you or disempower you. How to source our power from our Essence qualities is a need that went unmet in most of us. We learned the pseudo-power system of our defensive strategies. When you're present and resourced, you can respond from creativity instead of reactivity. But when your power was never mirrored to you as a child, you may unconsciously believe:

- *I'm powerless to change things.*
- *I can't trust my instincts.*
- *My presence has no impact.*

We often try to gain power by controlling others or proving ourselves. But this is a counterfeit power that leaves us exhausted. True power emerges the moment we validate our experience and reconnect with our Essence. That's when our nervous system shifts, our thoughts soften, and our creativity returns. From here our Essence qualities emerge spontaneously from within us to create experiences we want to have.

Take a Moment to Choose This Moment

Pause and place your attention on your unmet emotional needs for body/mind connection, a regulated nervous system, belonging, and power. Say aloud: "We were trained to believe our needs were wrong or too much. Notice openings and closings internally. The openings of hearing the truth and the closings of fear of unworthiness of such kind and understanding attention. Drop the truth—the truth about us is that we were always worthy of having our needs met." Notice how your body responds. Feel the shift in energy internally. That's your body, regulation, belonging, and power coming online from the inside out.

In the next section we'll explore more about how to validate these needs and reparent your inner self with Essencey value, compassion, and consistency.

Transforming begins with seeing yourself clearly. All of you, not just the parts you've been conscious of in the past. It's important you see your unmet needs, the powerlessness they cause, and the defensive strategies they activate not as flaws, but as sacred invitations to come home to your Essence.

PART II

Steps to Transforming Unmet Needs

CHAPTER 5

Generating Awareness

"Everybody thinks of changing the world; nobody thinks to change themselves."

—Leo Tolstoy

Previously, we connected with the healing power of Essence to heal unmet needs from the past. We're exploring how the fastest tool for shifting unmet needs or powerlessness is to validate to regulate. Now let's discover how unmet emotional needs, when misunderstood and then invalidated, can pull us into defensive patterns—and how to meet them where they are so they can transform.

You may have heard that as you age, it becomes harder to change your habits or that the brain is more plastic when you're young. While both statements hold truth, you can access your Essence qualities and re-wire your executive functioning at any age. Neuroscience shows us that the brain retains its plasticity across our lifespan. When we change something at a foundational level, ripple effects follow, shifting stuck patterns into opportunities for growth.

Stuck patterns are rooted in unmet needs, the stuck powerlessness they cause, and the stuck defensive strategies that try to overcome the powerlessness. We're learning there are many unmet needs, so learning the skills to meet these needs internally is life changing. Meeting the needs internally transforms the unworthy, unlovable, and unvalued aspects of us, so we can receive when others try to meet our needs. The transformation that comes from healing these unmet needs begins with shifting our perspective. This time, though, we're shifting our perspective, meaning our attention, inward.

Step 1: Shift Your Attention Inward to Increase Your Awareness

Attention focuses on specific stimuli, while awareness involves understanding what is happening internally and externally to provide context to our experiences.

Most of the time, we focus our attention externally, on the world around us and on the actions of others and ourselves. Shifting our focus inward means tuning in to our thoughts, emotions, and body sensations.

Very few of us were taught to notice our internal states first or to lovingly connect with our inner world before acting. But transformation starts with your internal experience. Over time, this inward focus reveals more and more of your inner reality.

Turning inward especially toward the body's experience is the most crucial step in this entire process. That's why you'll see the phrase "Notice how your body responds" more than 150 times throughout this book. (Are you listening, left brain? This step is for you! We need your help in making meaning of our body sensations instead of evaluating whether we should be having them in the first place.)

When shifting your attention inward, start by locating a part of your body that feels safe. I know, I know—if you're like most of us, you've never thought about locating a safe place inside your body. (Seems like an oversight, don't you think?!) Then engage your caring and curious observing awareness and place it in this safe haven. This gives you a grounded sense of self from which to explore other body sensations, even the ones that feel unsafe. For example, you might use the visual imagery of watching your body sensations onstage while you're seated in the viewing area of your solar plexus.

Being in observing awareness mode naturally creates a comfortable space between you and your experience. You become curious and creative, rather than consumed. This allows you to see the workings of your internal systems and patterns with clarity and choice.

Take a Moment to Choose This Moment

Notice your shoulders, your pelvic floor, your belly, your jaw, the back of your tongue, and any other areas holding tension. Bring Essencey energy—comfort, soothing, curiosity—to those areas. Ask, *Where is my attention habitually wanting to go when I feel these sensations? What sensations do I notice? Where do I feel openness? Where do I sense constriction?*

This is your very precious INTERNAL world—the origin of all lasting transformation, depending on how you treat it. Don't worry if you don't sense much instantly. With practice, your neural circuits will reconnect, allowing you to feel more of what's been happening inside.

Dissociation

Dissociation is a defense mechanism we learn early in life, often before we can speak. It happens when the right prefrontal cortex goes offline, numbing us to body sensations. You might think dissociation is extreme, but it's something all of us do daily.

Every time our sense of self disconnects from our observing awareness, we dissociate. Every time we rationalize with our left brain without checking in with the right brain's experience of the body, our left brain is dissociating from our right brain. Practicing the internal steps in this book will help rewire that part of your brain so it can reconnect with your body.

Here are some common examples of dissociation going on under the surface of everyday life:

- A father who can't access his feelings
- Someone who gets overly emotional
- Not knowing what you want for dinner
- Replaying conversations in your head

Everyone needs help with integrating trauma. If you dissociate, there was once a good reason for it. Asking for help is not weakness; it's a sign of powerful self-awareness. Consider working with a body-centered or developmental trauma therapist to support you in this journey.

Becoming aware of when you dissociate allows you to learn more about when you're in fear that you didn't realize was powerlessness fear. And every fear has an unmet need in it. Once you're seeing from outside your dissociation, you can recognize the stuck pattern and begin to transform it by validating the specific reason it was important to dissociate when you were young. Speak this *Simple Truth* to yourself: "I so appreciate you, dissociation, for keeping us safe from things we didn't have the capacity to understand and integrate when we were super-young." Notice your innerness.

Why is this so important? Because many of us were trained to dissociate as soon as we tried to give caring attention to our inner bodies. Validate to reassociate.

Discovering True Healing

Each time you give attention to your inner experience, you send a message to all the "younger yous" inside: *You matter/they matter.*

Curious, nonjudgmental awareness creates new neural pathways. When you validate your trained reactions and the remnants of pain they left behind, you release old stories held in the body. This process makes space for Essence to reemerge.

True healing happens when you give yourself what wasn't given to you. When caregivers operated in defensive mode, they couldn't access their Essence and unknowingly passed their fear-based patterns to you. Their projections of lack became your perceptions of lack. But you can change that now.

Take a Moment to Choose This Moment

Recall a time when someone listened to you with openness and love. That's what you're now doing for your insides.

Spend time in observing awareness whenever you can. Your right brain is where you comfort and soothe. Your left brain may resist connecting to the deep feeling right brain—here's why you should pay attention:

- To access your inner truth
- To shift internal states from defensive mode to Essence
- To amplify pleasant body sensations

Remember, your defensive training is not who you are; it's just conditioning that can be transformed. Essence is more powerful than any training.

Your sense of self was never meant to feel lack. Even when defensive mode is active, your internal resources remain. Resources are the antidote for lack. Reconnecting to your internal resources in moments of stress heals wounds and rewrites your memory bank. This is the Essence of transformation.

Take a Moment to Choose This Moment

Reflect on how you've responded from Essence and
how you've reacted from defensive mode. Recognize
the automatic reactions you inherited—and how they
shaped your relationship with fear, sadness, and anger
in your relationships. For example, notice how your
defensive strategies tend to select and train partners
who will reinforce your powerlessness beliefs. It's
tough to look at, but it has valuable information for
you about how your defensive strategies keep you
stuck in a hopeless cycle of pain even though they are
trying to keep you protected from other pain. Pursuers
pursue Distancers, Intellectualizers pursue Big Feelers,
and Self-Reliants pursue Dependents. All are defensive
strategies transacting with other's defensive strategies
activating each other's powerlessness fears. Awareness
is the first step toward change. Validate to transform
your relationships.

The Magical Power of Attention

Your attention transforms experiences. When rooted in Essence, you
gain clarity and creativity. When fused with powerlessness and fear,
your attention becomes rigid and limited.

Essence-based attention is expansive and generative—it seeks
what can be created. Defensive attention is protective and narrow—it
sees only threats and what you don't want.

Think of a moment when you were so engaged with life that time flew by. That's Essence-based attention. You're learning to give that kind of engaged attention to your insides. Tune into your physiology.

> You carry two physiological states, notice the difference moment to moment. Make this your practice:

- Essence-based (truth-aligned, settled, flowing)
- Stacked/defensive (threat-based, tense, disconnected)

Check out the graphic on the following page to draw your attention to your own internal world and why you may behave externally or feel internally in ways that you don't want.

You can sense how we fill our bodies and minds with Essence or defensive strategies. Bring compassion to yourself and others in this moment by remembering we do what we've been trained to do until we become aware of all the things going on inside that we didn't know were going on.

Your nervous system perceives threats through the lens of your Unconscious Procedural Manual. When old, unhealed unmet needs get triggered, your nervous system revs up or shuts down, fusing your sense of self with powerlessness.

In contrast, when you operate from Essence, you engage Stephen Porges's "social engagement system." You feel grounded, curious, and able to connect. Your body is relaxed, not tense. This difference in physiology tells you whether you're operating from Essence or from fear.

Where you place your attention determines your experience. Defensive mode and Essence create entirely different neural pathways. Essence integrates your brain and body, bringing the prefrontal cortex online, soothing the amygdala, and syncing emotional systems. Disintegration happens when the brain's systems have been trained to disconnect under stress.

Where Do You Normally Live?

Which one of these would you feel safe in?
Which one of these would you create what you want in?
Which one of these would you trust to protect you?
Which one of these would you rather play in?

STACKED

Withdrawing, Stubbornness,
Attacking, Withholding, Complaining,
Shaming, Blaming, Overpowering,
Rejecting, Coldhearted, Minimizing,
Justifying, Self-Righteous, Resenting,
Dreading, Closed-Mindedness, Giving Up,
Being Curt, Hoarding Resources,
Harshness, Numbing-Out,
Entitlement, Concealing, Guilting,
Controlling, Enmeshing, Biasing,
Intimidating, Being Moody,
Analyzing, Indecisiveness, Attacking,
Appropriating, Stressing, Repressing,
Vacillating, Hypervigilant,
Playing Small, Disregarding,
Constricting, Distancing, Impatience

ESSENCE

Composure, Alluring, Playful,
Affection, Daring, Curiosity,
Facing, Exploring, Giving,
Humbleness, Individuating,
Hoping, Loving-Kindness,
Marveling, Organizing, Soothing,
Willingness, Clarity, Collaborating,
Growing, Harmonizing, Wondering,
Trusting, Nimbleness, Modeling,
Inventing, Lightness, Mattering,
Loyalty, Originality, Peace,
Persistence, Wisdom, Validating,
Liberating, Liminal, Absorption,
Goodness, Sustainability, Integrating,
Movement, Reflecting, Strengthening,
Transforming, Simplifying,
Moment-to-Moment Creativity,
Equality, Dancing, Credibility

The perceptions, thoughts, and actions you fill your house (body) with have physical effects on you. We can perceive this in others as safe or unsafe.

Take a Moment to Choose This Moment

Ask: Am I filling my body with curiosity, wonder, and compassion? Or am I stuck in powerlessness and defensive mode, filling my body with fighty anger, blame, judgment, and criticism? If the latter, gently bring your attention back inside. Notice what's familiar about what you're experiencing. Familiar thoughts and feelings reveal stuck patterns of un-Essence. Strengthen your awareness muscle and reclaim your Essence. You will learn something new about yourself every time you look within if you do it from Essence.

Safety Resides in the Body

Real safety is a settled body. When you know your sense of self isn't threatened, your body relaxes back into Essence.

Our autonomic nervous system, located in our brain stem, is the part of us that perceives threats. It's designed to kick into either/or fast decisions to save life or limb. It wasn't supposed to be programmed with sense-of-self threats of unworthiness, but it was for many of us.

The brain stem also activates neurotransmitters like serotonin, dopamine, and norepinephrine. Neurotransmitters shift internal body states. Guess what activates them. Validations and Simple Truths, baby!

Powerlessness fear blocks these neurotransmitters from being released. Serotonin calms and soothes us. Dopamine motivates us to take actions we want to take. And norepinephrine revs us up into enthusiasm. Activating these is how we feel safety from within instead of trying to get others and the external world to stop scaring us.

Stress means the body is warning you about a perceived threat to your identity. We are not stressed about anything but sense-of-self threats. Validation of your experience can transform stress into safety. Validate to feel safe.

Take a Moment to Choose This Moment

Look at the Essence quality list again. Pick out ten Essence qualities that you know are really strong within you and appreciate yourself for these. Also appreciate your family of origin for cultivating these in you. Now pick out ten Essence qualities that you know are not as developed within you. Set an intention each day to cultivate, explore, and discover how to activate one of these Essence qualities within yourself. Notice and learn from other people you can see are strong in this Essence quality. Take a moment to turn within and invite this Essence quality to come forward in you until you can feel it as a felt experience. Continue to play, explore, and discover how to embody this Essence quality until you feel it automatically pop up through you one day. Then you know it's integrated. Appreciate, savor, and celebrate your diligence, determination, and fortitude to activate this very important Essence quality in you. Move on to another Essence quality and repeat.

Working Step 1: Applying Awareness Generators to Your Unmet Needs

Now, let's apply Step 1 by shifting our awareness inward, applying awareness generations to our unmet needs. These prompts help you reflect and collect information by making new connections you haven't made before.

Mind/body connection, regulated nervous system, belonging, and power are all needs that went unmet in many of us. Expanding your awareness about how your family treated these needs gives you insight into what you missed and what defensive strategies were passed down to you.

You might notice that you have a variety of Pleasers, Protectors, and Punishers inside that have the skill of a limited observing awareness and have been trained to use it through a fear-based lens of defensive strategies. For example, if you have a Protector, like a ruminator, a worrier, a hypervigilant, an obsessor, a skeptic, a critic, a read-the-room-er, or a super competent, you already know you have the ability to be the observing awareness inside of you. These defensive strategies are observing how you can be right or avoid doing it wrong. Awareness generators are a tool to retrain your observing awareness to notice your fear-based, limited observing awareness so you can transform it. Validations and Simple Truths also give you the pathway to transform (rewire) these defensive strategies back into your Essence-filled observing awareness. We will cover how to do them in the chapters ahead.

Mind/body connection awareness generators

(Within the parentheses are what people have answered before)

In my family of origin, we treated our internal body sensations _____

____.

(e.g., like they were nuisances; by giving them no attention whatsoever; like they were who we were; like they were good when everybody felt good about them and bad when others didn't feel good)

My mother's relationship with her internal body was ______________
____.

(e.g., totally shut down and dissociated; unknown; dismissed; happy when her body did what she wanted; revved up and out of control; fearful)

My father's biggest fear about his body was ________________________
____.

(e.g., that it took away what he wanted; that it was inadequate; that we came from unhealthy people; that it would break down)

My caretakers taught me my body was _____________________________
____.

(e.g., my head mover-around-er; just for movement or sports; the house of pain; a place to feel good when everybody felt good; where you feel bad about yourself inside)

My mother would get angry with her body when _____________________
____.

(e.g., it broke down; it didn't do what she wanted it to do; she felt pain; she was really afraid; she got sick)

My father gave attention to his internal body _______________________
____.

(e.g., when pigs could fly; when someone died; when he was sick; when he was playing the victim; never)

My caretakers treated my internal body sensations ___________________
____.

(e.g., like they were a burden; lovingly when they were happy sensations; like they didn't know what to do with them; like they were green aliens)

I'm realizing my training about how to relate to my internal body was
____.

(e.g., fear-based; nonexistent; full of animosity; to be happy inside when others are happy inside; confusing; inconsistent)

A simple action I could take to interrupt these patterns of relating to my internal body is ____________________________.
(e.g., appreciating my body; giving value to the difference between the training and what's always been true; bringing gratitude to the old strategies that kept me safe; choosing to trust that meeting unpleasant body sensations with Essence transforms them instantaneously)

My intention is to relate to my internal body experiences with ______
____.
(e.g., curiosity; compassion; love; empathy; sense-of-self empowerment while I feel; tenderness, nurturance)

Regulated nervous system awareness generators

My nervous system gets revved up when ____________________
____.
(e.g., I'm in connection; when I start speaking; when I'm listening to others) *List as many triggers as you can. There's usually a lot here. Take your time.*

My nervous system gets shut down when ____________________
____.
(e.g., I perceive someone making me wrong; I think too many thoughts about what others think of my actions; I go into self-conscious mode) *List as many triggers as you can. There probably will be more than you think.*

When my nervous system gets revved up or shut down, my sense of self experiences ____________________________________.
(e.g., a threat; chaos; unworthiness; nothingness; emptiness; a black hole)

One way I could calm my nervous system from the inside is to _______
____.
(e.g., have a conversation with my little kiddos inside; give value to my current internal experience; locate myself as the observing awareness of the information my body is giving me; meet my nervous system with Essence)

When my nervous system is settled, my sense of self feels ____________
____.
(Pick any Essence quality.)

Belonging awareness generators

One way I try to help myself feel that I belong (or that I don't need to belong) is ____.
(e.g., I say things I don't believe so I can fit in; I tell myself I can just ignore the need to belong because it brings up too much pain of disappointment; I convince myself that if I give to others, they will give back to me in the same way)

Another way I try to help myself feel that I belong (or that I don't need to belong) is by ____.
(e.g., shaming/shoulding others if they don't include me; saying, "I don't need them anyway!"; turning off my connection to caring)

My fear about belonging is ____.
(e.g., I don't have what it takes inside to belong; once I have it, it will go away; I'm not enough; I'm too much; the price is too high; I must lose myself to belong with you)

One way I could validate my powerlessness fear about belonging is __
____.
(Hint: Use the Validation *Yes, we were trained to believe* ___________.)

One way I could speak a Validating Truth to require my powerlessness fear to transform is ____.
(Hint: Use the Validating Truth *The truth about us is* ____________.)

One simple internal action I can take to connect more deeply with myself is ____.
(Hint: Notice how your body responds to create a mind/body connection. Mind and body connected equals a feeling of belonging. Fascinating!)

Personal power awareness generators

One way I transact for power instead of feeling it internally is by ____
____.
(e.g., comparing myself to others; judging others as less than; trying to be needed by others; trying to get others to prioritize my needs over theirs; acquiring material things as proof of my power; getting other people to do things the way I want)

One thing I noticed about my parents in power struggles was ________
____.
(e.g., my mom tried to feel power by controlling what my father did or didn't do; my father tried to feel power by believing his opinions were always right and other people were idiots; my father gave his power away as the way to feel some kind of power that he could stay in approval and connection; my mother used her anger as power)

One way that my thoughts disempower me is ____________________
____.
(e.g., my Protector tells me I should do something, and then I feel guilty unless I do it; my Pleaser tells me I must behave in a certain way to get other people to approve of me and want to keep me around; my Punisher tells me I'm so stupid for saying that thing I said in the meeting)

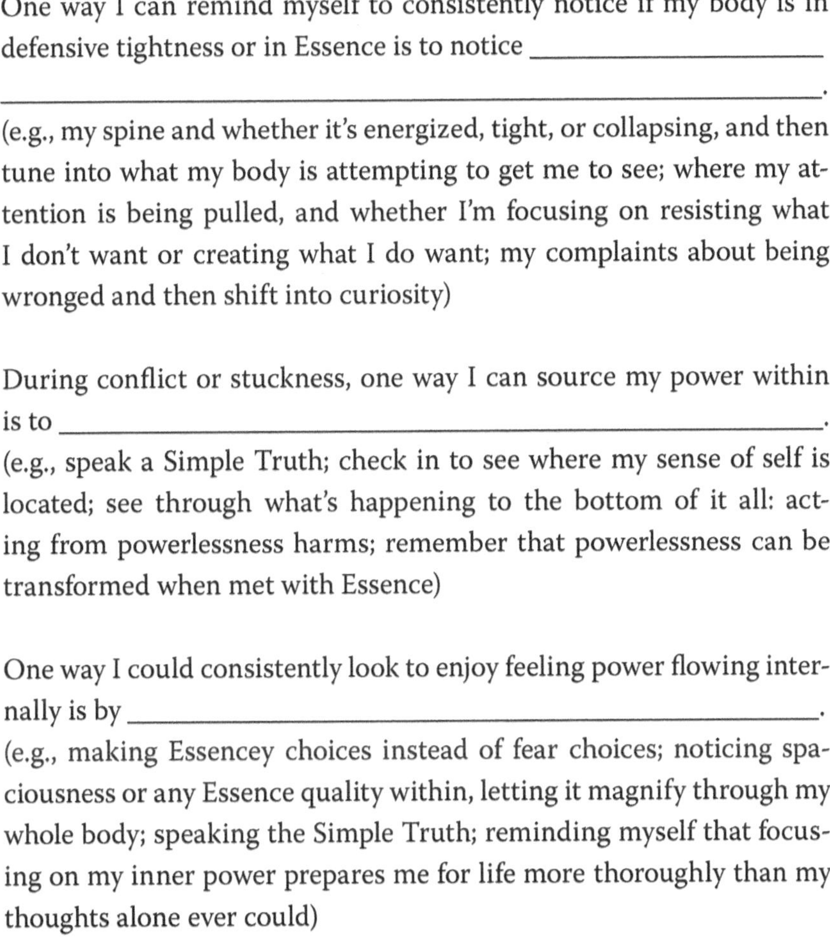

One way I can remind myself to consistently notice if my body is in defensive tightness or in Essence is to notice ____.

(e.g., my spine and whether it's energized, tight, or collapsing, and then tune into what my body is attempting to get me to see; where my attention is being pulled, and whether I'm focusing on resisting what I don't want or creating what I do want; my complaints about being wronged and then shift into curiosity)

During conflict or stuckness, one way I can source my power within is to ____.

(e.g., speak a Simple Truth; check in to see where my sense of self is located; see through what's happening to the bottom of it all: acting from powerlessness harms; remember that powerlessness can be transformed when met with Essence)

One way I could consistently look to enjoy feeling power flowing internally is by ____.

(e.g., making Essencey choices instead of fear choices; noticing spaciousness or any Essence quality within, letting it magnify through my whole body; speaking the Simple Truth; reminding myself that focusing on my inner power prepares me for life more thoroughly than my thoughts alone ever could)

When our sense of self fuses with our powerlessness body sensations, it changes our perception drastically. We lose our valuable skill of awareness. We go from seeing the world clearly to seeking relief from our fears. When our sense of self fuses with Essence qualities, it changes our perception into seeking inner truth. Imagine the difference between facing a misunderstanding from Essencey truth and reacting to a misunderstanding from defensive strategies. Validate your experience just the way it is showing up to expand your awareness about what's really going on inside. Validate to activate awareness.

CHAPTER 6

Validations

Previously, we explored how unmet needs shape inner patterns and how to generate new awareness about stuck fear-based patterns. This chapter dissolves the stigma around having needs, feeling unworthy, and talking to yourself. (Giggle.) We'll learn how validating these intensely uncomfortable and vulnerable experiences transforms them back into power. Validate to empower.

Step 2: Validate Your Internal Experience

The first step to transform was to expand your awareness about all your inner nooks and crannies. The second step in the transformation process is to acknowledge and validate what you find when you shift your attention inward. Validation is the act of giving value to what's currently happening inside you. It helps distinguish between the truth of your Essence and the conditioning or training you've received.

Validation is a need that went unmet for most of us. When this need goes unmet in us, it leaves a severe imprint of powerlessness to feel like our inner experience—our feelings, thoughts, body sensations, impulses, perception, and Essence—has any value. We feel not good enough, unworthy of interest and curiosity about who we are. Our Pleasers, Protectors, and Punishers kick in to try to make us feel valuable at the same time that we're already feeling not valued, splitting our energy into draining one direction and trying to force it into another. So, no matter how hard they try, and our defensive strategies do try hard, they can never convince us for sure that we do matter. Learning to validate our own insides meets the needs that went unmet and transforms the powerlessness beliefs back into the truth about ourselves.

A very transformative Validation begins with the phrase *Yes, we were trained to believe . . .*

For example: *Yes, we were trained to believe we couldn't make sense of our internal painful experiences.* Or *Yes, we were trained to believe we are responsible for other people's feelings.* Notice how your body responds when you say these to yourself. Making a distinction between your training and the truth about you transforms a lot of stuck fears in those past versions of you. It's a great way to connect with parts of you that you haven't known how to connect with before.

Most of us were taught to tighten against sensations we don't like, rather than acknowledge and validate all our feelings, *including* the uncomfortable ones. When we judge or avoid our internal experiences, we block ourselves from understanding what lies beneath them.

Sense-of-Self Threats

Here are examples of beliefs you may uncover when you look inward:

- *I'm not good enough.*
- *What I want doesn't matter.*
- *I'm unlovable.*
- *No one cares about my experience.*
- *I'm unseen.*
- *I'm doing it wrong.*
- *I can't do anything right.*
- *I'm unknown or unheard.*
- *I'm incapable or failing.*
- *I have no value unless I meet others' needs.*
- *I'm powerless to create what I want.*

Once you identify the threat, validate it:

- Yes, we were trained to believe that being right made us worthy of love.
- Yes, we were trained that what we want doesn't matter.
- Yes, we were trained to be at the effect of others and events instead of creating what we want. (We can't relax and be us because someone or something is doing this or that thing.)

As you say these Validations, step into your observing awareness and notice how your body responds. Does it relax, tighten, soften, or hold tension? Whatever you feel, allow it. Speak to those sensations with compassion: "It's okay for you to be here. I know you just want to be understood." Feel the power of comforting and soothing your experience as the way to transform feelings.

Validation Heals Powerlessness

Validation brings truth back into the nervous system. It tells the younger versions of yourself living in your memory and body: "You were trained to believe something untrue about your worth." Over time, these distinctions rewire your Unconscious Procedural Manual.

Value in the moment

Nothing shifts until it is accepted as it is. Acceptance means saying, "This is happening. How do I choose to face it from Essence?"

The goal is to keep your prefrontal cortex online while feeling powerlessness, tightness, or resistance. As you do, you'll start to experience yourself as the observing awareness watching what's happening inside, rather than identifying with it. Remember how we were trained to fuse with our feelings. This is you unfused. This shift is transformative.

Validating your internal experience helps develop your Essence voice, the one that soothes your nervous and emotional systems. This allows your attentional and identity systems to settle too. In this relaxed state, your body processes and releases old memories, making space for new ones.

Validating others when they're Stacked

One of the greatest gifts you can offer another person is presence. Not to fix or advise, but to validate what they're feeling in the moment.

Many of us were trained to interpret another's incongruent energy as a threat. As a result, we learned to focus on what's wrong rather than connecting to the human underneath.

Important distinction: Validating someone's inner experience is not the same as validating their opinion, belief, or behavior, especially their victimhood.

Here are some examples:

- Validating an opinion: "Your ideas make sense." (Not authentic if you don't believe it.)
- Validating an internal experience: "You really want to be heard." (Creates authentic connection.)
- Validating a belief: "Maybe it just wasn't meant to be." (Doesn't feel good to anybody.)
- Validating internal experience: "You feel disappointed. You really cared about this." (Conveys you're tracking their experience to understand.)
- Validating an idea: "That's a smart plan!" (May not like the whole plan.)
- Validating internal experience: "You're accessing your creativity and ingenuity." (They get to feel you valuing them even if you don't like the idea so much.)

You don't need to agree with someone to validate their experience. Instead, speak to the human need underneath what's being expressed. For example: "You value independence." "You want your body to be yours to govern." "You are showing how much you care."

This draws out their Essence instead of engaging their defensiveness. Validations impact minds and bodies by opening up to see from different perspectives. Real connection comes from shared humanness—not shared beliefs, ideas, or opinions.

Sometimes, it may take more than one Validation for the other person to feel safe. I often try three times. I call it the Law of Three Validations. Defensive strategies often initially perceive Validations as making them wrong. The Validations and Simple Truths still get through, the defensive strategy just might not be able to allow you to see it in that moment. If the defensive strategy is still holding on after three validations, take some time and revisit it later. I can remember so many times that people's truths stayed within me, working on me in there and helping me transform even though I couldn't show them at the time.

When people feel seen, their defenses soften. If you compliment someone from your head, it's one thing. If you take a moment to tap into your feeling for yourself and another and validate from your feeling in that moment, it intensifies the impact. We can tell the difference in each other.

Validate Yourself First

You can't offer authentic Validation to others until you practice it with yourself. Your unmet needs didn't go unfulfilled because you were unworthy; they went unmet because your caregivers didn't get their needs met either.

As you validate and transform your own powerlessness beliefs, you'll be less activated by others' defensive strategies. There is a ton of freedom and power in this skill of not taking defensive strategies personally. This creates more space for conscious choice, authentic connection, and the zesty joy of taking the high road of your core values during conflict.

Simple Truth: More Essence = Fewer Defensive Strategies = More Delightfulness.

Model the Behavior You Want to Receive

When someone is stuck in defensive mode, the best way to respond from Essence is to take responsibility in the way you wish *they* would. Instead of trying to convince them or correct their perception, which they can't do while in the defensive state, model the behavior you hope to receive. Your example becomes the mirror for their self-reflection.

Sample Validations: Reminder—you will only be able to say these to others after you validate to regulate your own insides.

- "I know there's a way for us both to get what we want. Let's shift into that mode."
- "You want me to hear something that's not feeling good to you. Let's slow down so I can really hear it."
- "I would never want you to feel that way. I can do something different."
- "Your experience matters to me."
- "There's a lot happening for me. Let's pause. I see more clearly when I slow down."
- "I want to understand you. Can you say it a little differently so I can hear you better?"
- "This feels like some stuckness between us. Let me come back into my Essence and respond from there."

Take a Moment to Choose This Moment

Validation gives value. When people feel valued, they start squirting serotonin, dopamine, and norepineph-rine out of their brain stem again. (Giggle—not exactly how it works but close enough.) Once the internal state transforms, the perception transforms. Stop efforting to get them to see what they are doing. Validate their Essence, and they will do all that work themselves. Whatever you give value to, you'll get more of it. Give value to someone's defensiveness by engaging with it? Get more defensiveness. Give value to their Essence? Get more Essence.

Working Step 2: Validate to Transform Unmet Needs

When you validate the difference between your training and your truth, your authenticity emerges. These moments dislodge stuck powerlessness and create in-the-moment shifts into Essence.

Over time, using Validations rewires your brain, specifically your prefrontal cortex, to stay online during conflict or stress. This supports your ability to embody the truth of who you are while others' defensive strategies are comin' at you with untruths.

Sadness emerges when we validate the parts of us that didn't get validated. It's very important that if you feel sadness emerging when you validate the training you received that you take a few moments to reorient yourself in the present moment by feeling your feet on the ground or looking around the room or space you're in and identifying a few objects on either side of you. Since our sense of self was trained to fuse with our feelings and body sensations, it's easy to get pulled back into the middle of them when they arise. Locating your sense of self in the present moment as the observing awareness interrupts this pattern. Let's practice.

Mind/body connection Validations

Validation: "Yes, we were trained to believe our mind is more valuable than our body in helping us know who we are."

Notice your chest and belly. Are they relaxing, tightening, or a mix of both? Feel the truth land in your body.

Validation: "Yes, we were trained to believe that the pain of powerlessness in our body is who we are."

Notice how your body responds. You might feel tightness at first that then releases. If you feel nothing, it's okay. You may have learned that your body was the place where pain lived. Many of us dissociate from our pain. Over time, these Validations will help you reconnect so you'll be able to feel your body sensations more easily. I couldn't do this at first at all, now I'm the Queen of Validations! Giggle.

Regulated nervous system Validations

Validation: "Yes, we were trained to believe we can't trust our internal experience to help us because it's too busy hurting us." Notice your heart rate. Is it shifting? Do you feel hot, sweaty, or disconnected?

Validation: "Yes, we were trained to believe that the way to regulate our fears is by defending our sense of self against attacks." Notice your inner energy. Is it flowing or stagnant when you validate the training?

Belonging Validations

Validation: "Yes, we were trained to believe our ability to belong depends on how others see or treat us." Notice your body's response. Is there fear of exclusion or contraction, or a desire to disconnect?

Validation: "Yes, we were trained to believe that there are parts of us that don't belong, so we need to disconnect from those parts of us." Notice how your body responds to acknowledging these parts. You might experience a mixture of expanded-ness and contraction. Watch both and see what they do next. Your feelings are not overwhelming if you're observing them instead of being them.

Personal power Validations

Validation: "Yes, we were trained to believe that power comes from how we control the external world, not from our internal world." Notice sensations like queasiness, shame, or heaviness. These are signs of powerlessness asking for transformation.

Validation: "Yes, we were trained to believe that the way to get our needs met was to overpower others or underpower ourselves." Notice how your body responds. Power feels like energy moving, and powerlessness feels like energy getting stuck. Be the observer.

Final Thoughts on Validations

Validation isn't just a nice thing to do; it's a powerful way to retrain your mind and heal your nervous system. Speaking Validations to your inner self welcomes back all the parts of you into wholeness and brings you back into presence.

Notice what your unpleasant body sensations do when you validate them. Unpleasant body sensations open up and melt away. And yet, notice how giving Essencey attention to pleasant sensations expands them, magnifying them into more pleasantness throughout the body. Our body unleashes its intelligence when our mind connects to our body.

We've been taught that validating someone's unpleasant experience will somehow "reward" or prolong their discomfort. They'll get more stuck in victimhood, sadness, or fear if we validate them. The opposite is true. When someone's internal experience is known and valued, the unmet need is met—and they naturally shift into Essence.

This is one of your superpowers: Validation instead of evaluation, to get your needs met and to meet the needs of others. Met needs mean no more powerlessness and defensive strategies. We're then free to create instead of reacting. Saaaaaweet!

CHAPTER 7

Simple Truths

Previously, we learned that needs are not a sign of weakness but were often not empowered by Validations. We learned that validating the training and the truth creates clarity by regulating the nervous system, connecting the mind and body, and cultivating inner states that honor that all parts belong. This empowers us by connecting the past and the present so our actions in the present are no longer ruled by our past. Now we explore the universal needs that shape all human experience—and how you can meet them with Essence by learning to speak Simple Truths.

We've explored Step 1 of generating awareness by connecting current stuck experiences to their origins in kiddohood. We began our mastery of Step 2 by learning to validate to transform stuck unconscious beliefs. Now it's time to get truthful.

Step 3: Speak Simple Truths

Simple Truths give value to a current experience—yours or someone else's—without making anything or anyone right or wrong. Our bodies automatically relax and let go when we hear the Simple Truth. To do this, you must tap into your extraordinary moment-to-moment creativity. We feel most alive when we are creating in the present moment.

Being spoken to with Simple Truth is a need that went unmet in most of us. The who's-right-who's-wrong system has often replaced speaking the truth in our overall culture. We needed our caretakers to know how to change our unwanted behaviors by speaking a Simple Truth to us instead of judging our behavior as right or wrong. If this need went unmet in you, you would feel a powerlessness about whether you're doing things right or wrong and whether your sense of self is right or wrong. Your Pleasers will try to do things the way other people say is right. Your Protectors will talk you out of taking risks or convince you to take too many risks so as not to do it wrong or to rebel against other's rightness. Your Punishers will punish others and yourself for not doing things right, the way your upbringing taught you was right. The right-or-wrong system is an attempt to know what's true without accessing the truth internally.

Simple Truths begin internally. Start by tuning in to your body. Notice where any tightness resides. Then speak a Simple Truth to that tightness as if you were offering compassion to a powerless part of yourself. For example, "I appreciate the heck out of you, tightness, for letting us know there's powerlessness fear in the system right now." Or "Receiving Validation for who we are on the inside is so different we aren't sure if we can trust it yet."

Notice how your body responds to this Simple Truth. It may flourish with sensations briefly and then settle. That's transformation beginning. This Simple Truth responds to the unmet need of not being valued for your current experience. When you value your current experience, it shifts on its own.

Speaking Simple Truths to yourself locates your awareness outside of your reactivity. It calms both your emotional and nervous systems. Try expressing them aloud. My trick is to put earbuds in so people think I'm on the phone. (Giggle.) Let your mind get interested in how your body responds because that's an instant sync-up of mind and body. You'll notice how soothing it feels when your internal experience is met with compassion instead of judgment.

Essencey attention sends a clear message: It's safe to be here. When done consistently, this cultivates deep trust in your ability to guide yourself through any experience. Speaking Simple Truths builds connection with your inner truth and cuts through defensive strategies. Simple Truths cut through the bull pooey. Who doesn't want that?!

Simple Truths vs. Validations

While they overlap, Validations focus on recognizing your conditioned responses ("Yes, we were trained to believe . . ."), while Simple Truths reflect core truths that bring healing, insight, and authenticity (for example, "It's scary to disidentify with your thinking mind.").

Simple Truths also stimulate your vagus nerve, especially the ventral vagal branch, which regulates your autonomic nervous system (your sense-of-self alert mode). Many of us never learned how to activate this pathway. But Simple Truths can get it working again.

Take a Moment to Choose This Moment

Creating your own Simple Truths is a powerful experience. One way to generate them is by identifying your defensive strategies—like judgments or justifications—and then identifying the unmet need they're trying to meet. For example, if you're judging and saying, "They should see through that person as a liar," distill that down to "They're seeing through either/ors, which limits what they let themselves see." Or "I'm spending so much time justifying my defensive strategies instead of creating something new in this moment." Notice how your body feels different when you generate Simple Truths compared to judging or justifying. You might notice yourself taking a deeper breath. Judgments and justifications keep your mind locked into either/ors that are keeping you stuck in reacting to what you don't want instead of creating what you *do*. Both/and it to create something new.

If your goal is to inspire self-reflection, not self-righteousness and denial, you're on the right track. Simple Truths linger inside and pull us toward our authenticity. They have impact internally, whether the current defensive strategy knows it or not.

Speak Simple Truths to Yourself and Others

Practice first by speaking Simple Truths to yourself. As you strengthen your ability to settle your own insides, these truths will begin to emerge organically in interactions with others.

Take a Moment to Choose This Moment

What would your day look like if you replaced judgment and justifications with Simple Truths? "I'm wondering how I'm not being curious and creative right now because of my judgments and justifications." How might this double checking yourself change not just your internal world but your external one too?

During conflicts or misunderstandings, one of the most important things you can do is fully drop into observing awareness. Most conflict can be traced to one person's powerlessness belief triggering another's.

Try this *Simple Truth*: "I'm not interested in making you wrong. I'm interested in creating change that works for each of us. I want to create from Essence."

Speak this to yourself first, especially if you're feeling defensive. Notice how your body responds. Identify whether your sense of self is fused with defensive mode. Ask: Am I seeking approval? Trying to avoid disapproval? Trying to be right? Emphatically making someone else wrong-er than they just made me? These are signs your Pleaser, Protector, or Punisher has lit up and knocked you out of Essence.

Remember the results that you want to create. Defensive strategies get very predictable results: power struggles, stuckness, disconnection, and unmet needs. Essence qualities get very creative results: transformation, understanding, empowerment, and deepening connections.

Speak Simple Truths to your insides first. For example: "I feel you in there, little ones. We were taught that being wrong meant we were failing." You might notice sensations of shame, tension in your stomach, or a tension behind your eyes—all signs of internal struggle to know what's true about you. Speaking Simple Truths engenders spaciousness, ease, flexibility, and the ability to respond instead of reacting.

In an instant, one sentence can destroy a relationship or transform everything: Turn *You only care about people who believe what you believe!* into *You show your caring through having the right way to do things.* There's an evaluation in the first and a valuing built into the second that safely soothes everyone and nudges the mind to open to new ways of caring. Speak Simple Truths to transform bodymind stuck Stacks first.

Working Step 3: Speaking Simple Truths to Your Unmet Needs

If Simple Truths were about just telling the hard truth, they would be called hard truths instead of Simple Truths. Hard truth has evaluations in it that activate nervous systems to not reflect on what you're expressing. Not the results you want! Simple Truths calm and soothe with their ability to clarify confusion, create safety during conflict, and convey what really matters. Simple Truths give value to what's going on at the foundational level of experience, calming nervous systems and opening minds. Simple Truths shift the paradigm from evaluations as the way to change behavior or belief to validating the need that is motivating the behavior or belief as the way to change it.

Mind/body connection Simple Truths

If you feel numb or tight, say, "I appreciate you, dissociation, for keeping us safe before we knew how to transform overwhelming sensations." Or: "Thank you, tightness, for letting us know we're scared to feel certain feelings like sadness, fear, or anger." Or: "I'm realizing our mind is not discerning the difference between our emotional reactivity and our present moment emotions." (Sadness as powerlessness fear about the self's worthiness compared to sadness due to loss of a cherished connection.)

Notice how your body responds. You're looking for openness or tightness in your torso. Notice how speaking to your body directly feels different from just thinking about it. The mind calls out, and the body answers. You don't want to miss your answers.

Here's another *Simple Truth*: "I'm integrating how we were taught to value using more words over noticing how our body responds to the words being spoken." Notice your insides.

Regulated nervous system Simple Truth

Simple Truth: "I'm putting together how much of ourselves has been hidden from us." Or: "I'm realizing feeling different inside can mean something good is happening instead of something bad." Or: "I'm putting together how powerful we feel when we regulate our nervous system by speaking Simple Truths to calm our powerlessness fears."

Rewind the tape, after each of these previous Simple Truths. Notice how your body responds to a warm and wise voice emerging from inside of you. You might get the sense that your body is trying on the new experience. This might show up as tension that dissolves into relaxation. That's cool. Let these truths support your feeling of connection to Essence resources inside. Notice how you can feel safe and powerful instantly by learning to regulate your nervous system from the inside out.

Belonging Simple Truth

Simple Truth: "This powerlessness is here to be integrated and transformed back into our wholeness where it belongs." Or: "I appreciate you, tightness, for showing us how deeply we long to belong." Or: "I'm integrating how our fear of not belonging requires us to override our authentic yeses and nos."

Repeat the ones that resonate with you. Notice how your body responds. Sadness emerges when fears subside. Speak a *Simple Truth* to it: "I feel you, sadness. I know you are the sadness of feeling unworthy of belonging." Notice how your sadness (heaviness and tightness in your chest, throat, and eyes) responds to being invited to belong.

Simple Truth: "I'm realizing we feel like we belong whenever we feel our Essence resources inside, regardless of whether others treat us a certain way." Notice your body's internal experience. You might experience lightness or buoyancy inside. Maybe a tingling of energy moving.

Personal power Simple Truth

Simple Truth: "I feel gratitude for you, tightness in our belly, for showing how afraid we've learned to be of our internal power." Or: "This powerlessness is not our sense of self. It's a trained-in experience." Or: "I'm realizing whenever we're using defensive strategies, we're in powerlessness underneath."

Notice how your body responds to these. You might feel thrumming or humming pulsations of energy inside. You might notice a freedom and ease of energy moving inside. The time you take to notice your insides is valuable because you are teaching yourself a new way to engage with your own power inside. When you notice your insides, you connect to your Essence qualities and then act, think, and express from them.

You can also speak directly to your defensive strategies: "Thank you for kicking in so fast to try to turn the power back on." Or: "I appreciate the heck out of you, overcontrolling Protector, for instilling a power in us before we knew how to feel real power from our Essence resources inside."

Notice how your body responds. Notice where energy feels like it's moving in your body and where energy feels like it's stuck. Energy moving feels powerful to us, and energy stuck feels like powerlessness.

This skill of noticing body sensation activates the parts of your brain that can transform your powerlessness fears by disidentifying with them and identifying with your Essence.

If you've caused harm with your past versions of power (as we all have), speak the truth: "We're committed to learning and growing. When we expand our awareness through learning, we are transforming harm into healing." Notice your body's shifts internally as you speak to yourself.

Simple Truths validate instead of blame. We aren't making our parents or our pasts wrong; we're naming the patterns so we can transform them. Doing so gives us power to create new experiences. Simple Truths are like fist pumps for your own insides. Feel the power, spread the Simple Truth.

Now it's time to explore a special kind of Simple Truth, Validating Truths. Read on, curious reader, to hone your skills of dropping gems of truth that have the power to transform.

Validating Truths

Previously, we explored how to speak Simple Truths. We learned that Simple Truths and Validations are emotional and nervous system regulators. When they are dysregulated, we distort reality. When they are regulated, we perceive reality clearly. We learned to use these terms interchangeably most of the time and occasionally in specific ways. This chapter reveals how to validate the truth that has always existed inside of us once the powerlessness belief has been validated. Validating Truths follow a Validation after the Validation has created the opening for the Validating Truth to be believed.

The steps we covered so far:

- Step 1: Generate awareness about how the past is being reenacted in the present through a stuck powerlessness belief.
- Step 2: Validate the unmet need that the powerlessness belief represents. Locate yourself as your compassionate observing awareness inside.
- Step 3: Speak Simple Truths to the little past versions of you that went through what they went through, meeting the need that didn't get met previously.

Step 4: Speak Validating Truths

Validating Truths are a specific form of Simple Truths. They begin with the lead line "The truth about us is . . ." Their purpose is to resonate with the truth that already exists inside but has been obscured. Validating Truths are only spoken AFTER an untruth, a powerlessness belief, has been validated. They are paired with Validations. In this section we separate them to focus on how to express them and how they work. If you try to speak the truth about yourself while the powerlessness belief is running, you won't believe it. After your body recognizes that the training you received is not the truth, it is open to accepting what's always been true about you. Examples include:

- "The truth about us is our sense of self is inherently good because our Essence qualities are our inner goodness."
- "The truth about us is our defensive strategies don't know how to trust our Essence qualities to handle the moment."
- "The truth about us is who we are was never who our parents' defensive strategies saw."

Notice how your body responds. Your body experiences a realization as wholeness, grounded-ness, and stillness. You can feel an expansion of your inner self to fill out all your spaces inside and even beyond your skin boundary. You may also feel tightness. Speak a *Simple Truth* to the tightness: "I feel you tightness. I know we were trained to be fearful of our goodness, Essence, and power." Notice how the tightness responds.

Validating Truths are spoken after you or another have shifted from powerlessness to power. If you speak a Validating Truth before you've validated the unmet need, it feels invalidating to the recipient. We unintentionally convey to each other that we shouldn't be having the experience we're currently having when we do this to each other. We've all been trained to do this via our Pleasers, Protectors, and Punishers. Trying to pseudo-validate each other's experience by "making it better" with devastating mistiming.

When you speak a Validating Truth to yourself and then place attention on your body, your nervous and emotional systems begin to resonate with pulses of pleasant energy we identify as truth, happiness, hope, connection, wisdom, and empowerment (all Essence qualities). This is you experiencing your Essence qualities in the moment.

This is how you step off the who's-right-who's-wrong playing field and into internal truth-based grounded awareness. It's a truly transformative skill, to feel truth in your body so clearly that you are no longer confused by the untruths coming from another Stacked-up human or your own Stacked-up insides. To feel the truth so strongly it guides you through conflict and unknowns. To connect to your deep truth so pervasively you can trust you're seeing reality clearly.

Here are more examples:

- "The truth about us is we feel powerful and resourced when we give nonevaluative attention to our insides."
- "The truth about us is our sense of self is a creator of experience, not just a reactor."
- "The truth about us is we feel balanced and flexible when our left and right brains are integrated."

Remember to notice how your body responds after each Validating Truth. It seals the deal between your mind and your body, often spurring connecting memories or more Simple Truths.

Practice when you're calm to prepare for when you're activated. Eventually, these skills will become second nature. When you do get Stacked, you'll shift back into Essence more quickly.

This is how living from Essence becomes your new normal.

Absorption, Immersion, and Engagement

Another *Validating Truth*: "The truth about us is we can connect to Essence qualities inside of us that we didn't even know we had, and they are ready to go."

For example, absorption, immersion, and engagement are Essence qualities that drop us into the flow. Our defensive strategies do pseudo-versions of our Essence qualities like obsessing, efforting, and overcoming. The flow is when our body and mind are undulating in perfect sync. It feels like our internal creative intelligence is lining up with the creative intelligence of the universe, and we are in pure moment-to-moment creating mode. This creative spark gives each of us our unique sparkle, and our sparkle cultivates our moment-to-moment joy.

Once you learn to de-fuse your sense of self from powerless thoughts and feelings using Validations and Simple Truths, you can re-fuse with what you choose, like your Essence qualities. We can drop our full Essencey attention into our body and let ourselves get absorbed in our pleasant body sensations. Sensations that represent empowerment, moment-to-moment creativity, and competency feel really good to us. This kind of immersive engagement is what flow feels like.

We all move between immersion, absorption, and engagement in powerlessness fear or in our Essence qualities. Notice how your sense of self can feel consistent, even though it's bouncing around and fusing with different aspects of you inside. That's because the powerlessness fears run under your awareness until you bring them into your awareness, where they can start to feel not like you, but like training that you received.

For example, when I lift weights, if I immerse in the power of my body, riding the wave of energy being produced from within, the set flies by. But if I resist what's happening by getting absorbed in *This is hard!* thoughts and feelings, the weight seems heavier than usual, and the set drags on seemingly forever. In that moment, my sense of self can fuse with resistance or power. Feel the power—spread the word internally! We can have a lot more power over our experience than we were trained to have.

Another real-life example

Recently, construction outside my office window became so loud I felt invaded. My body tightened. I wanted to yell at those inconsiderate nincompoop hammerers and yammerers. Fighty anger kicked in—an old pseudo-power pattern erupted where my Essence had been only moments before. My Punisher. The part of me that wanted retribution for my pain released the Kraken.

But now I knew another way. I validated the underlying belief: "No one ever attunes to our experience." That shifted me back into observing awareness. I spoke soothing Validating Truths: "The truth about us is we can center our attention in creativity instead of in resistance to what they're doing."

My inner experience transformed. The noise faded from the front of my awareness to the background of my awareness. Who knew we could do that?! I didn't even hear it anymore. This shift would not be possible without great effort if I hadn't validated the attention-pulling powerlessness belief. The Validation freed up my attention. I felt free to focus on my clients. They would comment on the noise that I had completely forgotten. I learned how much our minds get stuck focusing on what we don't want to be happening because our powerlessness can't let it go.

Take a Moment to Choose This Moment

Close your eyes and take a few Essencey breaths, relaxing up and down your spine all the way to your pelvic
floor muscles. Reflect on some times when your activated
powerlessness beliefs pulled your attention, engaging
your awareness in what you didn't want to be happening.
Speak a *Simple Truth*: "Validating our experience frees
up our attention to immerse ourselves in focusing on what
we do want." Notice how your body responds. Notice
energy flowing and energy stuckness. Validations, Simple
Truths, and Validating Truths round out the emotional
feeling cycle that needs to be completed to free up your
attention. Imagine how your daily life might shift if you
guided yourself with an Essencey voice inside instead of a
fear-based voice. No one told us our Pleasers, Protectors,
and Punishers were fear talkin' inside our heads.

Practice speaking Validating Truths multiple times a day. Especially when you're *not* triggered. This retrains your Unconscious
Procedural Manual to be threat-free. Next time you're activated, you'll
respond with more ease and presence.

Getting Present While Activated

This means locating your sense of self as the observing awareness
within your internal safe space even when your body is activated. This
is the foundation of transformation. It shifts your identity from fusing
as the fear to fusing with your Essence.

Working Step 4: Speaking Validating Truths to Unmet Needs

Mind/body connection Validating Truths

Validating Truth: "The truth about us is our mind needs our body just as much as our body needs our mind."

Notice how your body responds. Feel expansion? Tightness? Transformation happens in the noticing.

Now, validate your thinking mind: "I soooo appreciate you, thinking mind, for working so hard to find the experience we want in the outside world." Notice your you-know-what.

Each time you bring loving attention inward, you build new neural pathways. Over time, you'll naturally choose this Essencey path.

Validating Truth: "The truth about us is our wholeness is dependent on our mind valuing our body's responses to what it generates."

Notice how your body responds. Notice how much letting-go can happen in your body when your mind and body are in sync. You might notice body sensations of spaciousness and lightness.

Remind yourself that your powerlessness sensations are not you—they are stuck patterns asking to be transformed.

Regulated nervous system Validating Truths

Validating Truth: "The truth about us is our observing awareness can regulate any internal experience—whether we're revved up or shut down."

Notice your body's response. You may feel expansion or contraction. If fear arises, validate it: "We were trained to believe that no one cares about our needs." Notice how your fear responds.

Validating Truth: "The truth about us is regulating our nervous system with Validations and Simple Truths interrupts our dependence on the external world to be a certain way for us to feel safe and powerful."

Notice how your nervous system responds. Back in the window of openness?

Belonging Validating Truths

Validating Truth: "The truth about us is our sense of belonging comes from our internal connection to our Essencey resources inside."

Notice how your body responds. Do thoughts arise? They've been trained to. Do they try to pull you into your head and away from your experience? This is part of the process—just notice it and return your attention to your body sensations.

Validating Truth: "The truth about us is we can feel like we belong even when we're excluded if we check in with our inner truth."

Notice how your body responds to the realization that all of you, even your fears and defensive strategies, want to feel like they belong to the wholeness of you. You might notice a rush of energy in your torso or a tingling feeling inside. Revelations feel like bubbling excitement and a letting-go of tension at the same time.

Personal power Validating Truths

Validating Truth: "The truth about us is our power resides in our ability to choose from our vast internal Essencey resources inside."

Watch how your body responds. You might notice an uplifting wave or energizing around your spine. You are repatterning your nervous system for flow and ease where there used to be tightness and fear.

Validating Truth: "The truth about us is we can experience power in our body as energy moving freely."

Notice how your body responds. You guessed it. You're looking for energy moving freely.

Final Note on Validating Truths

Simple Truths Validate; they do not blame. You don't need to make your parents or past wrong. But you do need to name the patterns to transform them. Validating Truths empower you to do just that.

When you validate a stuck pattern and then follow it with a truth, you liberate your body from powerlessness.

Remember, Validating Truths are most powerful when spoken after your body has shifted from powerlessness to resourced. If spoken too early, even truth can feel invalidating. Watch for timing.

The essential practice is shifting your sense of self into your observing awareness. You're cultivating an Essencey-voiced observing awareness inside that validates what has always been true about you. This is how you integrate and heal trauma.

In the beginning, practice this when you're calm. As you strengthen your skill, you'll be able to access it even in difficult moments. Over time, it becomes your new normal.

When you get Stacked (and we all do), you'll be able to shift back into Essence with increasing speed. You're learning the internal actions to take.

PART III

Awareness Generators to Transform Unmet Needs

"Healing begins where the wound was made."

—Alice Walker

CHAPTER 9

Abundance

"When you realize there is nothing lacking, the
whole world belongs to you."

—Lao Tzu

Previously, we named and validated some powerlessness beliefs for the unmet needs of mind/body connection, regulated nervous system, belonging, and power.
We've been exploring and integrating how Validations,
Simple Truths, and Validating Truths reconnect us to
our internal pathways, where we can experience these
needs as worthy. Embodied in this worthiness, we can
have the experience of power, belonging, feeling,
self-regulation, and mind/body connection internally

> as our safe base from which to create ourselves anew
> moment to moment. Now, in this section, we'll learn
> about some other common emotional unmet needs that
> also caused disintegration of our sense of self. In this
> chapter you'll learn how internal abundance is the anti-
> dote to fear-based insecurities and an important part of
> your path back to your sense of self in Essence.

It's important to know how to experience internal abundance so you can experience more external abundance. The ability to source internal abundance so we can perceive external abundance is a need that went unmet in most of us. If this need went unmet in you, you would have a powerlessness belief imprinted in you about abundance that is not the truth about abundance. Let's say you have a powerlessness belief that resources are always lacking—there's not enough time, sleep, energy, understanding, etc. . . . Your Pleasers, Protectors, and Punishers will be striving to get resources while simultaneously feeling like there is never enough. In this powerlessness cycle, nothing ever feels like enough.

Abundance is knowing that there are plenty of resources to go around, not through rose-colored positivity but through authentic experience. When you're in touch with your inner Essence resources, your external experience shifts.

When you're having a fulfilling internal experience, your need for external Validation diminishes. And, ironically, when you're feeling valid internally, others validate you more because they can see your value. You're living it. You can feel equally nourished by sitting quietly beside a brook, landing a big promotion, or waiting in a long line. These experiences are different, but each can be fulfilling when grounded in Essence.

The pandemic closed down many of our options. I lost access to activities that once filled my days and was left feeling alone, isolated, and robbed of something I couldn't name. Eventually I realized: I missed novel experiences. The external sources of novelty and connection were gone, and I slid into victim powerlessness perception. I was at the effect of the pandemic. I had been trained to seek experience externally instead of creating it internally.

So, I set a new intention: to treat each moment's experience as novel because of the resources I brought to each experience. Simple Truths in question form become Essence questions: "How could this allegedly trite moment be enough?" As the Essence questions shifted me into the present, my body softened into ease and flow. Then came another Essence question: "What experience do I want to create right now to feel abundance?" Every answer came from within. My favorite was deepening my capacity to love what's right in front of me. The simple perception of enough resources creates the internal experience of abundance.

We've been trained to believe we're powerless to perceive or trust that there is enough for everyone to get what they want. What do we all want? Essencey experiences.

Common powerlessness beliefs include:

- *Either you get what you want, or I get what I want, but not both.*
- *Abundance comes from outside of me.*
- *Abundance is how I'm rewarded for being good.*
- *There's always something lacking.*
- *Resources are limited. I won't get what I need.*

Take a Moment to Choose This Moment

Write down some perceived lacks in your life—maybe it's not enough love, time, energy, or jeans that fit. Validate that your need for abundance matters: "We were trained to perceive resources through a fear-based lens of not enough by our caretakers' defensive strategies." Notice how your body responds. Then speak Simple Truths about the abundance of resources you're learning to perceive internally: "I'm realizing when we get scared about external resources we're already disconnected from our internal resources." How does your body feel now? Our body sensations generate internal states that influence perception. When people are disconnected from their internal resources, they perceive lack both inside and out. When we're hooking up with our own innovative insides, we perceive abundance. This feels like the true secret to manifesting what you want. Create it through internal actions first. Then the external creative intelligence can match it.

We are trained to see what's missing—time, money, safety, support. These patterns of external lack come from an internal disconnection from Essence. In this state, we constantly search externally for something or someone to meet our needs. But those needs can only be transformed into worthiness when fully met internally.

This outward orientation makes us excellent consumers, but not very satisfied humans. Travel may feel like freedom. Possessions may feel like Validation. Attractive partners may feel like worthiness. But learning to meet our deep internal needs connects us to our inner abundance and transforms how we experience the world.

Abundance Awareness Generator

Reflect on each prompt and complete the sentences. Sample answers are provided:

When I perceive I'm being thwarted, my defensive strategies kick in and automatically ________________________________.
(e.g., resist the thwarting; knock me out of Essence; rev my nervous system into alert mode)

My defensive strategies limit my perception of abundance by ________
________________________________.
(e.g., narrowing my view; playing the victim; convincing me I can't get what I want)

I can tell my defensive strategies are active when I hear voices in my head saying ________________________________.
(e.g., it's either my way or the highway; either we're right or wrong; I'm an idiot)

One way I can catch and shift from lack perception is by ____________
________________________________.
(e.g., speaking a Simple Truth to the fear; reminding myself I'm disconnected from my internal resource department)

One way I can build capacity to create from my internal resources is by ________________________________.
(e.g., practicing embodying warmth; cultivating the Essence of completion; trusting that Essence will emerge when I show up)

Take a Moment to Choose This Moment

When you're perceiving lack, pause. Get curious. What
did your family focus on—abundance or lack? Notice
what your body tells you. Let memories emerge, not to
help you blame but to understand where your perceptions came from. Making these connections with your
past is part of the transformation.

Validating Your Trained-In Experience

Validation: "Yes, we were trained to believe that we need to act, perform, or accomplish in a certain way to receive abundance."

Notice how your body responds. Feel the openness or tension in
your chest, back, and abdomen. When your inner kiddos feel seen,
your body expands. Give value to all of them, including your two-year-
old and your six-year-old. Even your fourteen-year-old!

Speak this *Simple Truth*: "I'm learning how much our perception
of our internal abundance of Essence resources authenticates our external actions."

Notice your body's response. You might feel a sense of grounding in your spine and feet. When grounded in Essence, the world feels
more supportive, and you feel more capable.

Validating Truth: "The truth about us is that abundance is an inside
job. It transforms our perception so we can experience, express, and
produce Essencey actions."

Notice what tightens or relaxes. Appreciate whatever emerges,
like fear, sadness, or anger, and greet it with curiosity, warmth, and

attunement. Your body sensations hold wisdom about the training that shaped you and the truth waiting to emerge.

The need for abundance is met when we are taught to recognize the internal resources already within us. If your caretakers did not validate this, you can now activate this system yourself by learning to validate your own insides.

Abundance is yours. Your transforming resources are inside of you, not out there. You've always had access to them; they just needed your Essencey attention to come alive. Validate to experience abundance.

CHAPTER 10

Choice

"I don't ask for the sights in front of me to change,
only the depth of my seeing."

—Mary Oliver

Previously, we rooted into your internal Essence resources to experience your internal abundance. This chapter helps you work with emotional triggers—signposts pointing you to unmet needs like choice and your next layer of healing.

Your life is one choice after another. Every moment of every day, you are making choices. Even *not* choosing is a choice. Being taught that we always have the power to choose is a need that often goes unmet. If this need went unmet in you, you would have powerlessness beliefs about your power of choice that aren't the truth about you. Your Pleasers, Protectors, and Punishers will have all kinds of strategies to make choices or not make choices that get in the way of getting this need met.

For example, your Protector might convince you that you have no choice, so you let someone else make the choice. Your Punisher might kick in and resent the heck out of their choice, while your Pleaser smiles away like everything is A-okay. Since your Punisher can't let it go, it keeps stewing inside of you, until you blurt out how selfish and inconsiderate the other person is for making the choice you offered them to make. Oh boy!

Victim powerlessness is the belief that we don't have choice. Victim powerlessness perception is blaming our alleged lack of choices on others or external events and waiting for the transformation to happen outside of us.

When you are in Essence, the choices you make resonate throughout your body. They arise from within, often surprising you with their clarity and truth. Knowing what you want and acting on it from Essence gives you access to a powerful and renewable source of energy. Choosing to go inward before taking outward action is one of the most foundational and powerful choices you can ever make. It's the choice to source safety internally, freeing yourself from the exhausting attempt to control your external circumstances.

Essence-based choices are creative and aligned with what is true in the moment. Fear-based choices stem from old familiar stuck patterns that often result in frustration or suffering due to their lack of creativity. True safety comes from choosing interoception (nonjudgmental looking within and tending to your internal state) along with exteroception (the nonjudgmental scanning of the external world for information or cues to sense what's happening). Compare these to their defensive versions, hypervigilance (where sense-of-self fear is motivating an evaluative surveillance) and rumination (where we're going over and over things internally, looking at ourselves and others through the who's-right-who's-wrong lens so we can figure out how we're not the wrong one).

We've been trained to believe we are powerless to know what we want with clarity. Powerlessness beliefs that interfere with making clear choices include:

- *I can't trust my choices.*
- *I don't know how to know what I want.*
- *It's safer to let others decide.*
- *My choices matter more than yours.*
- *I could make the wrong choice.*

Take a Moment to Choose This Moment

Write down the powerlessness beliefs you hold about making choices. Become intimately familiar with them so you can recognize them when they try to hijack your sense of self. Do you make choices before checking in with your current body state? How do your Pleasers, Protectors, Punishers, or powerlessness voices override your truth about your choices?

Pleasers say, "I can handle it, while others can't." Protectors say, "We must limit ourselves or others to be safe." Punishers justify their actions—"I'm mad as hell, and we're not going to let this happen to us, AGAIN!!!" Powerlessness says, "I have no choice." These voices carry your inherited programming of *have to,* not your Essence truth of *choose to.*

Validate each part for trying to meet your needs the best way they knew how. When your body starts to soften and open from being validated, your truth can emerge within the openness.

Much of your choice-making process was shaped by how your parents made, respected, or rejected choices. One client, Ted, realized he equated needing help with weakness. No one had taught him how to make empowered choices. To feel powerful, he convinced himself he didn't need others and built pseudo-power through intellect and emotional distancing. His free-to-be-me power of choice was converted into choosing to not need.

Once Ted gave himself permission to explore this pattern without blame, he saw how limiting it was. He had passed it on to his children without realizing it. Ted's internal safety system had been built on defensive strategies. Once he validated that system, he could shift to making choices from true safety sourced within his observing awareness. From here he made the courageous choice to repair this with his kids by owning what he had unknowingly passed down and validating the harm it had done to their ability to make choices. Imagine hearing this from your caretakers. Generational transformation, so cool. By the way, the true generational wealth that you can pass down is Essence.

Most of us have been trained to make choices from fear. Even when someone appears powerful, their choices can be rooted in fear. Essence-based choices freely share power with others. When I need to extract power from someone or something, I'm already operating from a place of internal fear and victim powerlessness perception.

If your sense of self is perceiving a threat, your reality is already being distorted by fear and its contraction of the mind and body down to either/ors. Either/ors are choiceless because only one end of the polarity is considered right. Choices made from this place do not satisfy because they're built on avoiding fear, not creating from truth.

Empowering Internal Choices

- Choose how you view your thoughts and their meaning.
- Choose thoughts that empower rather than drain you.
- Choose to locate your sense of self in Essence, not fear.
- Choose to relate to your internal experiences with compassion.
- Choose which Essence qualities to develop.
- Choose to self-reflect until your truth emerges.
- Choose to create instead of suffering.
- Choose to increase your capacity to love.

Examples of shifting from fear- to Essence-based choices

⚠ Fear: "I'll feel better if I just get it done."

♡ Essence: "I'm choosing to face this task with moment-to-moment creativity and curiosity."

⚠ Fear: "Don't speak up; nobody listens."

♡ Essence: "My experience matters. I will express it in a way that bypasses defensive strategies."

⚠ Fear: "This isn't fair. I'll demand my way."

♡ Essence: "I'm choosing candor, consideration, and co-creation."

⚠ Fear: "People are idiots."

♡ Essence: "Others are making fear-based choices. How might I be doing the same?"

⚠ Fear: "I deserve this!"

♡ Essence: "Am I trying to fill an internal void? What Essence quality do I truly want to experience?"

Take a Moment to Choose This Moment

Step into your most curious self and explore the patterns behind how you were trained to make choices. Write down three fear-based choices and their Essencey counterparts. Come on, write them down. Make the choice to do something different from the usual. Make the choice to have the experience now. It shifts your internal experience by focusing your attention more deeply. Integration comes from having the experience, not thinking about it. Integration means you have embodied the concept, and it is yours to use in your life. Choose you.

Choice Awareness Generator

Reflect and complete:

The training I received from my father about making choices was ___
____.
(e.g., my father taught me rebel choices: If no one saw it, it didn't happen; you must demand that people do things; you have to sacrifice your choices; it's safe to let others make choices for you)

The training from my mother was _____________________.
(e.g., only one person gets to choose for everybody; you let the opportunities come to you, and you don't create them; you can manipulate people out of their choices by questioning them)

My father treated my mother's choices ________________________________
____.
(e.g., like they were limiting; with resentment; like they were equal to his; like they were work-arounds; like they were special)

My mother treated my father's choices ________________________________
____.
(e.g., like he knew best; passive aggressively; with respect; like they were the introduction to an argument)

My parents treated my choices ________________________________.
(e.g., like they were less important than theirs; with respect when they were in alignment with their choices; as if they didn't exist; like they were invalid; like they were negotiable)

Another influence on my choices was ________________________________
____.
(e.g., watching my parent's choices fail or succeed; watching how my parents treated my older sibling's choices; watching my parents condemn other people's choices as idiotic or stupid)

Some fear-based choices I now recognize are ________________________________
____.
(e.g., distracting myself from what I say I want to do; blaming others when things don't work out the way I want; stepping out of my integrity by breaking agreements I make with others; disempowering myself with my thoughts and not catching it)

My fear-based choices keep me stuck by ________________________________
____.
(e.g., believing their limitations are legit; believing that safety comes from not choosing; limiting my perspective to either/ors; keeping me in my head and missing my body's cues)

My body responds to fear-based choices by ________________
____.

(e.g., tightening up big-time; shutting down into confusion; getting rigid inside like my thinking; bunching up my pelvic floor)

A simple action to make Essence-quality choices is ________________
____.

(e.g., asking myself what a specific Essence quality would do in this situation; choosing interoception to notice my body sensations when I choose; reminding myself of the results I get with Essence and fear choices; validating my feelings first)

A way to tap into Essence when choosing is by ________________
____.

(e.g., catching my Pleaser, Protector, and Punisher voices and validating their effort; noticing my familiar victim powerlessness perception and validating that was then [the training we received] and this is now [the truth about us]; listening to the wisdom in my body by noticing how my body responds to different choice options)

My body responds to Essence-based choices by ________________
____.

(e.g., dropping into ease and flow; offering up novel Simple Truths spontaneously; coming into alignment with my wholeness; connecting my mind and body so I feel connected to everything)

Deepening Choice Awareness Generators

I often make external choices before internal ones by ________________
____.

(e.g., speaking or acting before I've checked in with my internal experience; not noticing my Protector has hijacked me into catastrophizing and I'm acting upon its counsel; forgetting to locate my sense of self internally)

To better notice my internal state, I can ___________________________

____.

(e.g., set an intention to train in Essence breathing as my default state; set a timer every thirty minutes to notice if I'm in tightness or ease and flow inside; express a *Simple Truth* like "My insides determine my perception")

To catch limiting meanings I assign to events, I can ________________

____.

(e.g., notice when I tell myself the story that no one cares; catch my *It's too hard*; bring awareness to what I put off that I know I want to do; notice when my thinking activates my not-good-enough heaviness inside)

A more powerful meaning I could assign is ___________________

____.

(e.g., that others are in fear when they are doing harm; does this choice create energy moving or more stuckness; how can I transform this; how can I notice and transform the right or wrong playing field by speaking Simple Truth; understanding instead of evaluating)

Validating Your Trained-In Experiences

Validation: "Yes, we were trained to believe our choices make us fearful instead of powerful."

Notice how your body responds. Some inner kiddos may tighten with fear, trained to believe they'll be wrong if they choose what they truly want. Validate their fears based on the training they received.

Simple Truth: "I'm realizing our fear of being wrong leads to more fear-based choices."

Notice your body. Even if there is still fear, a bunching up in your belly, some part of you will settle when the current experience is validated.

Validating Truth: "The truth about us is our choices can be experienced as separate from our sense of self."

When you locate as your observing awareness, your choices become learning opportunities. You stop making your internal experience wrong.

If you feel tension, speak this *Simple Truth*: "I'm realizing how many choices we've made in defensive mode."

Notice how past versions of you respond through body sensations. You might feel sadness or fear that your younger parts don't yet trust this new way. You're teaching them to trust you by considering their experience.

Another *Simple Truth*: "I'm realizing how important internal choices are in connecting us to our Essence."

Notice how your body responds to the awareness that internal choices are a pathway to freedom, clarity, and authenticity. Let yourself feel the ease and power of making choices from this Essence-based inner space.

Our choices are so valuable because nothing and no one can take them from us. We can feel the power of our choices unless we have fallen into victim powerlessness perception where we believe the story that someone or something can take our choices away. When we were young, our caretakers' defensive strategies could take our choices—and therefore our power—away. That's what imprinted the powerlessness in us in the first place. As adults, though, we get to take our power back by validating that if we are telling ourselves we have no choice, we are having a momentary invasion of the past into our present. We can bring ourselves back into the present by validating the difference between our training and the truth about us. Validate to feel the power of your choices.

CHAPTER 11

Appreciation

"I was never addicted to one thing; I was addicted to
filling a void within myself with things other than
my own love."

—Yung Pueblo

Previously, we unpacked the role of powerlessness beliefs
as fear or Essence guides to your choices. We explored
how your choices either empower you or disempower
you. Now we trace your learned patterns of appreciating
and being appreciated for your Essence—how unconscious criticisms in your past trained you to disconnect from
Essence—and how to rewire this training so when someone's defensive strategies criticize you, you can ground in
your truth that they are seeing you through their fears.

Notice how our unmet needs imprinted powerlessness about these Essence qualities. Yes, all the unmet needs listed are Essence qualities or inner pathways to connect to Essence qualities. When the need for appreciation goes unmet in us, it prevents us from having access to that Essencey resource during times of stress, conflict, or unknowns. Right when we need access the most!

Appreciation is a need that went unmet for many of us. You can tell whether your need for appreciation was met by observing how you try to get your needs met. If you appreciate to get your needs met, that need was likely fulfilled. If you criticize or try to control instead, then appreciation may have been missing in your upbringing. You will have a powerlessness about being appreciated and not trust appreciation as a powerful resource to get your needs met.

Your Pleaser will appreciate others, and your Punisher will judge them for not appreciating you. Your Protector will convince you not to appreciate others because it makes you too uncomfortable and awkward. None of this is true about you, but we all believe it when these defensive strategies are babbling away inside our heads. We need to cultivate an Essencey voice in our heads that can transform these well-meaning but distorted voices of our defensive strategies.

Appreciation and attention are closely linked. Appreciation includes attention, but attention doesn't always include appreciation. Appreciation means intentionally noticing what's good, what's working well, or what's been overlooked that deserves value. It's the internal act of giving value to what we want more of.

Appreciating your internal experience is what allows you to act FROM your internal goodness because you conjure it up when you appreciate it. Appreciating each other's internal experience is how we become better humans together by reflecting each other's Essence back to each other. And once you recognize that every person has both Essence and defensive mode within them, it becomes easier to see beyond someone's defensive strategies behavior and notice their Essence trying to emerge.

What would happen to our relationships and our culture if we led with appreciation of each other's inner goodness as the way to cultivate wholeness? When people feel their wholeness, they create change that respects the wholeness of others and the planet.

Take a Moment to Choose This Moment

Write down five things you appreciate about yourself. Now write five things you appreciate about a close relative or partner. For a deeper challenge, write five things you genuinely appreciate about someone you perceive as a "villain" in your life. Your goal isn't to justify their actions or make them a better person but to take them out of the villain role in your inner world. This sets you free from them.

Many of us were taught to criticize, reject, or guilt others into changing rather than appreciate who they are. When we're appreciated only for our external behavior, not our internal experience, we learn to value appearances over authenticity. But what we deeply crave is appreciation for our Essence, not for performance.

Criticism, control, and guilt activate defensive strategies, not true connection. And when we're in defensive mode, nothing feels truly satisfying because we're disconnected from our Essence.

Take a Moment to Choose This Moment

Reflect on a recent situation where you responded with criticism instead of appreciation. Now rewrite that interaction as if you had spoken from appreciation. How does this change the results you get?

I had a huge epiphany when I realized I was using criticism to get my needs met. I didn't know then that when we connect to our Essence, caring for others comes naturally, and that criticism makes it nearly impossible for others to stay connected to their caring for us. I also didn't know that my own beliefs about unworthiness were fueling the fighty anger criticisms I was bringing into situations.

I needed to learn how to appreciate my inner Punisher for trying to protect me from the despair of unmet needs. I needed to validate my powerlessness so I could witness it transform. That's how I began meeting my inner moments with Essence instead of reactivity. Warning: Results may vary depending on whether we use defensive strategies or Essence.

Appreciations create a bicycle wheel of awareness of good will, and criticisms cause a bicycle wheel of lack of awareness and ill will.

Some common powerlessness beliefs related to appreciation are:

- *No matter how hard I try, I won't be appreciated.*
- *No one appreciates me.*
- *I give and give, and no one gives back.*
- *There isn't anything about me worth appreciating.*

A great resource on the art of appreciation is the Hendricks Institute. Gay and Katie Hendricks offer valuable tools, books, and trainings to support your appreciation journey. I appreciate these two innovative leaders for their courageous and creative pursuit of Essence. Gay for your outrageous authenticity, and Katie for your infinitely mystical empathy. Thank you for saving my emotional life.

Appreciation Awareness Generator

Reflect on these statements:

One way my defensive strategies keep me from appreciating myself is by ____.
(e.g., focusing on external achievements; telling me I can't appreciate myself until I'm perfect; making me uncomfortable when I try to appreciate myself or others, causing me to forget I can transform my discomfort)

One way my defensive strategies keep me from appreciating others is by ____.
(e.g., my Punisher not knowing how to appreciate to get more of what I want; convincing me it's just too uncomfortable; convincing me I won't do it correctly; telling me the story that I don't have the right words)

One way my attention gets pulled into criticism instead of appreciation is by ____.
(e.g., my Punisher kicking right in without me noticing; forgetting to check in with my body to see if energy is flowing or stuck; trusting my criticizer more than my Essence; my belief in the story that my appreciator can't get my needs met)

One way my attention gets pulled into control or justification instead of appreciation is by ____.
(e.g., my self-focused Pleaser or Protector voice can get me so focused on my pain or upset I don't notice other's experience at all, let alone

appreciate them; my Pleaser voice tells me I can't think of anything else to say but *Thank you and I believe it*; my Pleaser feeding me very believable justifications and loopholes as the truth; my Pleaser being too busy covering up what we're doing wrong to notice what others are doing right; my Punisher, who's too busy guilting or shaming others into behaving in a way that's easier for me, than being able to appreciate them for who they really are; my Pleaser telling me only what I want to hear or see about myself; my Punisher voicing demands that my needs have priority over others' needs, and then my Protector voice feeding me justifications about my ongoing non-Essencey behavior)

One way I could teach myself to get comfortable giving appreciations is by ____.
(e.g., remembering I can transform my automatic eruption of discomfort using internal actions; practicing giving appreciations to my own Essence qualities as they show up, so I trust myself when giving them to others; using the defensive strategies list and the Essence qualities list to discover what Essence qualities the defensive strategy is attempting to mimic and appreciate the Essence quality attempting to emerge)

Appreciations are a very effective way to get what you want without all the defensive drama. You're not just practicing a skill; you're rewiring your nervous system and reestablishing your relationship with your Essence. Appreciation isn't fluff. It's transformation.

Validating Your Trained-In Experience

Validation: "Yes, we were trained to believe that we are only valuable when we behave a certain way and that external performance is the only way to be appreciated."

Notice how your body responds. Does it open, constrict, or feel sad, scared, or tense? Whatever arises, appreciate it. Your body is telling you about your experience. If your body begins to settle, bring your attention there and allow the sensation to expand. You're turning on your observing awareness.

Speak this *Simple Truth*: "I appreciate you, body, for clarifying what our actual experience is."

Notice your body's response. How does it feel to be appreciated for the invaluable skill of simply showing you what's true inside?

Speak another *Simple Truth*: "I deeply appreciate how valuable our internal experience is to our sense of self."

This inward attention is how you align with your truth. It's how you connect your mind and body, so they work in harmony instead of opposition. Without interoception, they operate out of sync.

Validating Truth: "The truth about us is that our internal experience is valuable and worthy of appreciation because it impacts our external behavior."

Notice how your body responds. Do you feel warmth in your chest? A heaviness of shame? Fear in your belly? Each sensation matters. It may be signaling memories of old pain surfacing. Be kind to these feelings because they are not who you are. They are memories of past pain.

When you place your observing awareness behind your experience—inside your body but outside of the reactions—you help fear settle. Your body can tell when it's receiving Essencey attention instead of fear-based attention. Defensive attention keeps it activated. Essencey attention soothes and transforms.

Speak this *Simple Truth*: "I'm discovering that if we appreciate our internal experience, it transforms. Our perception of the external world shifts, and we're free to act from Essence." Notice that amazing inner body of yours.

You're now giving your inner world the appreciation it needed when you were younger. Strongly tethered to your Essence resources inside, you can weather others' storms of defensive strategies. You can appreciate in the moment when you would usually attack or counterattack. Appreciations cultivate Essence to emerge in even the most non-Essencey places. Appreciation isn't a side hustle. If you make it your go-to for getting your needs met, getting your needs met gets a lot easier. Appreciations transform inner experience, which opens up perception. An open perception is flexible. Validate to access your appreciator.

CHAPTER 12

Vulnerability

"Vulnerability is the birthplace of connection and
the path to the feeling of worthiness. If it doesn't feel
vulnerable, the sharing is probably not constructive."

—Brené Brown

Previously, we saw how your training taught you to use
appreciation or criticism to get your needs met. We
learned appreciation is a need for all of us. It's also
a skill you can get comfortable with through practice.
This chapter explores your defense against your own
vulnerabilities—how they once helped you survive and
how you can compassionately retire them from their
current stuckness back into their own Essence.

Vulnerability often stems from the unmet need to have our authenticity validated. When authenticity is invalidated by others' defensive strategies, it creates a body-felt memory we experience as vulnerability to the threat of unworthiness, a form of powerlessness. If this need went unmet in you, you will go to great lengths to avoid the feeling of vulnerability. Our Pleasers are busy acting out our vulnerability. Our Protectors are convincing us not to go there or to overshare it. Our Punishers intimidate us and others right out of our vulnerability. We can spend our whole lives trying not to be vulnerable and miss out on knowing big chunks of our authenticity.

This feeling of vulnerability emerges when our usual defenses are down—when we're unguarded, un-Stacked, and exposed. But here's the powerful truth: Vulnerability is your deep Essencey spirit trying to live through you. It's your courage, your irrepressible life force, and your unshakable will to connect, grow, and express.

Those uncomfortable moments when you feel exposed are signs that your authentic self is breaking through. Your authenticity, unbeknownst to your defenses, doesn't need protection. It doesn't have to hinge on how others treat you. It can operate outside the right-wrong paradigm, where it's free to be itself.

Take a Moment to Choose This Moment

What inside of you feels vulnerable? What part believes
that if your guard is down, something bad will happen?
Locate a place in your body that feels safe. Imbue
this place with your wise, compassionate observing
awareness. From here, guide the vulnerable part of you
with a Validation it didn't get: "I know we feel intensely
uncomfortable because this part of us didn't get what it
needed." Notice your body's inner response. Envision
the vulnerable parts of you as those little past versions
of you that need to be accepted into the wholeness of
you. Let them know they are wanted, appreciated, and
safe to be genuine.

For years, I resisted vulnerability. I managed everything I said or
did to avoid that feeling. When I finally got curious, I imagined myself
putting on my magic wonder pants—silly, paisley pants with happy
mushrooms preening as they delight in exploring and discovering.
That playful image helped shift me into a state of wonder.

In this space of wonder, I realized I had been abandoning my vulnerable self, which gave me a clue: This part had been emotionally
abandoned. It feared being wrong, especially in contrast to someone
else being right. This vulnerability was stuck in the right-or-wrong
system. What did it need to transform powerlessness into power? Essence, of course.

When I met my vulnerability with compassion, an unexpected
thing happened: A little Joni emerged; sweet, innocent, and eager to
connect. I cried remembering her and reconnecting with her. She told

me there were other little Jonis stuck inside. I welcomed the journey to meet them all.

Why is this part of us so uncomfortable? Because it wasn't validated as kids. This doesn't mean we were unworthy; it means our caregivers weren't in touch enough with their own Essence to validate ours in certain situations, like when they were stressed.

Take a Moment to Choose This Moment

Express your vulnerability instead of avoiding it. Infuse it with Essencey power. From your observing awareness, guide your inner parts with nurturing, compassionate truths. Teach yourself to identify with your Essence voice rather than fear-driven inner gossip.

We've been trained to feel powerless when we experience vulnerability. Some common beliefs include:

- *My vulnerability is a weakness.*
- *My vulnerability won't get me what I want.*
- *My vulnerability will be attacked or I'll be abandoned.*
- *I can't stand feeling vulnerable.*
- *I am my vulnerability.*

Unchecked, vulnerability can turn into powerlessness. People who don't know how to relate to their own vulnerability will reject it in others—or abandon them for it. When vulnerability is validated, it becomes authenticity.

Vulnerability Awareness Generator

Read each prompt and reflect on your inner truth.

I feel most vulnerable when ____.
(e.g., I'm feeling feelings unexpectedly; I love; I've made a mistake; something I wanted didn't work out for me; I'm attempting to express how I feel, and the words don't come easily)

I've been trained to ____
whenever I feel vulnerable. (e.g., squirm!; hate it; feel eeeeeeexxxx-tremely uncomfortable; get fighty angry; yell; defend myself; escape)

One way I can interrupt this pattern is ____
____.
(e.g., I can see my vulnerability as a cry for help from my insides; I recognize that there are aspects of me inside that don't know how to trust our Essence as powerful; I can call out my automatic reactions lovingly and transform them in the moment, modeling what I want others to do also, so all involved are self-reflecting; I can speak a *Simple Truth* to my vulnerability: "I know you need to be met with Essence so you can transform into your authenticity," then notice how my body responds to being met with Essence)

One way I can transform my vulnerability into power is by ________
____.
(e.g., being present with it instead of running a defensive strategy over it; learning about the powerlessness belief it's trapped in; speaking a *Simple Truth* to it: "Our caretakers' defenses spoke untruths to our Essence, which imprinted these fears about our sense of self as wrong," then notice how my body responds; speaking another *Simple Truth*: "We didn't know it was untruth then; we know it now," then notice my body's response; meeting my fearing body sensations with some warmth and tender Essence instead of more fear)

One thing I can learn from my vulnerability is _________________.
(e.g., what happened to me as a child; what happened to my parents'
vulnerability when they were children; how to be kind and compassionate with the body sensations I've previously been afraid of, then I
can listen for the wisdom my body is sharing with me internally)

Validating Your Trained-In Experience

Validation: "Yes, we were trained to believe our vulnerability is a defi-
cit that cannot be transformed."

Notice how your body responds. Maybe you let go of something.
Or maybe you tighten. Just observe it with kindness from your observing awareness view. Listen to the memories that want to emerge.

Speak this *Simple Truth*: "Our feelings were never wrong, even if
they were treated as such." Notice what shifts. Remind yourself that
noticing and validating your internal experience is more important
than fixing or solving. Speak another *Simple Truth*: "We still feel vulnerable when we feel our feelings." Notice your you-know-what.

Allow yourself to appreciate and savor any pleasant sensations
that accompany this recognition.

Speak this *Simple Truth*: "Our vulnerability is a fear of feeling
powerless, incapable, inadequate, or unlovable."

Notice how your body responds to this clarity. Notice and savor
any sadness that emerges. This sadness is trusting you to validate it
with your presence as the observing awareness. These sensations are
not you; they are trained-in patterns surfacing to be transformed.

See if you can feel power in disidentifying with these feelings and
patterns and reidentifying with your Essence, so your identity as your
Essence is guiding your old identity as powerlessness.

Validating Truth: "The truth about our vulnerability is our body sensations are messages from our Unconscious Procedural Manual saying, *Please transform us back to authenticity.*"

Notice your body's response. Is it opening or still hesitant? Either way, locate yourself in your Essence as the observer.

From there, listen to what your vulnerability is afraid of and speak a *Simple Truth*: "I know this feels like a part of us that no one wants to help." Notice what happens in your body when your body hears a truth.

Your vulnerability isn't something to banish. It's a part of you craving Validation because it didn't get it. As soon as you offer value to this part of you, it begins to transform. Meet your need to feel valuable by appreciating the authenticity hidden in your vulnerability. With every validating, Essence-infused internal action you take, you build trust that your vulnerability can, and will, transform. Validate to transform your vulnerability back into your authenticity.

CHAPTER 13

Unconditional Love

"Once you realize you can do something, it would be difficult to live with yourself if you didn't do it."

—James Baldwin

Previously, we explored your defenses to being vulnerable. We learned we can transform vulnerability by validating it instead of avoiding it or acting it out. We also discovered why it's important to transform your vulnerability, because it has your authenticity stuck inside of it. Next, we're going to explore how Essence and defensive strategies love differently. You'll learn how internal Validations melt fear and empower every part of you to move toward your wholeness.

The need for unconditional love cannot be met by even the kindest defensive strategies. Our people-pleasers try to be unconditionally loving but don't know how to source love from within. They only know how to transact for love externally.

Unconditional love is given from one's Essence, so you need to be connected to your Essence internally to feel it or express it. Unconditional love is experienced in the body as openness, warmth, and free-flowing energy. You can experience unconditional love within your body at any moment by giving value to your current internal experience. Essence qualities give unconditional love.

Our need for unconditional love often went unmet by our caretakers' defensive strategies, leaving an imprint of powerlessness in our Unconscious Procedural Manuals about our lovability. If this need went unmet in you, you would feel both the unworthy powerlessness of being unlovable and the lack of capacity to unconditionally love others. Check in curiously with your Pleasers, Protectors, and Punishers. Learn about what tactics they use to strive to be unconditionally loved so you can teach them how to be authentic about loving.

Most of us don't know how to love because our Pleasers, Protectors, and Punishers are confusing the heck out of us about our lovability and how to be loving. Our Pleasers are offering love to be loved so love becomes a transaction. Our Protectors are convincing us not to be loving or to be overloving so we can never be hurt by love. Our Punishers believe in tough love, which means withholding love if someone is not behaving the "right" way. Maybe you can sense now how our defensive strategies and trained-in beliefs about love activate our powerlessness to feel loved by each other.

Unconditional love is revealed when you step into yourself as the observing awareness behind it all. As the observing awareness, you can love even when you're not being loved. You can give understanding when you're not being understood. You can continue creating the experiences you want to have, even when others are reacting to experiences they don't want to be having.

Idealization means projecting onto someone qualities that you need them to have—whether they have them or not. For many years, I confused idealization for unconditional love. I went through many cycles of idealizing and disappointment in relationships, searching for unconditional love and trying to force it on a person. If I could just get them how I needed them to be, then I would get the unconditional love I was worthy of. Understanding how idealization was my attempt to get unconditional love created two responses: the joy of realizing something valuable for my future relationships and the despairing devastation of having chased a fantasy version of love my whole life.

This burst of insight at once shattered and reconstructed me into expansion, warmth, and fluidity, and I innately knew this was unconditional love I was experiencing for myself. Then my head kicked in and said, *Wait, how did we get here? We've got to memorize how to do this!*—and promptly knocked me right out of it. (Giggle.) As it often does, thinking about the concept knocked me out of the experience.

But the realization had integrated enough for me to understand that unconditional love meant holding two opposite feelings within me at the same time: anger and caring, joy and despair, hatred and love, forgiveness and justice, surrender and ambition. This is the both/and experience we can feel internally. My defensive either/ors can't do this. This realization expanded my awareness of the importance of always connecting to my internal Essence qualities. If I'm sourcing from my Essence, I'm sourcing from unconditional love. That's the place where I can do both/and instead of either/or.

Take a Moment to Choose This Moment

Contemplate a time you felt unconditional love for yourself. Most of us weren't taught to hold two opposites within us at the same time. For example, grace and awkwardness, power and innocence, and especially love and frustration. Today, practice bringing an Essence quality to a non-Essencey experience you're having and notice what happens when the two meet internally.

Loving unconditionally doesn't mean you give up your needs. It means you intentionally bring love to the places and players inside where you haven't before (like your Punisher or your powerlessness). Your practice of unconditional love displays your belief that love transforms your insides first, so from this loving place, you can transform what's going on around you. For example, if you set the intention to connect to your loving presence when you're angry, your anger helps you speak up, while your loving presence conveys warmth, dignity, and grace in your approach.

We've been trained that our Essence alone is not worthy of unconditional love.

Some of the powerlessness beliefs that accompany this include:

- *Love means approval.*
- *I have to be a certain way in order to get love.*
- *There are parts of me that are bad and unworthy of love.*
- *Love always goes away in the end.*
- *Love always comes with strings attached.*
- *Love means pain.*

The two versions of us inside either inspire or contrive two vastly different experiences of love. Our Essence gives and receives unconditional love, which looks like openness, acceptance, warmth, and respect to get needs met. Our Stacked defensive version gives and receives conditional love, which is manipulative, controlling, overpowering, or judgmental to get needs met. Our defensive strategies can justify withholding love. When we hear ourselves saying things like, "They need to learn their lesson," or "They don't deserve my vulnerability," that is pseudo-love with strings attached.

This training runs deep. We are taught to need others to give us love and approval without realizing what we really need is to unconditionally love and approve of ourselves. We spend a lot of time manipulating each other to try to get our needs met, and in doing so, we give and solicit conditional love. This comes from fusing our sense of self with our defensive strategies.

Take a Moment to Choose This Moment

Turn your mind inward and cultivate unconditional love within you right now. Contemplate how hard it is to be human sometimes. Our dreams, our ideas, and our hearts get crushed. Identify yourself as the unconditionally loving observing awareness capable of bringing love to the parts of you that wonder if they're lovable when things go wrong. Hover here until you can feel the parts of you that need love—the little ones who didn't get it. Generate warmth in your chest and surround the tense parts of you. Speak this *Simple Truth*: "We were always worthy of unconditional love, even when our caretakers couldn't give it." Notice your response.

Trying to take the right actions to receive approval is very different from taking the right action from Essence. Parents can only teach children to trust in their Essence qualities if they are in their own Essence while doing the teaching. Remembering that these unconscious patterns were trained in us early helps us have compassion for ourselves and others. Teaching yourself to love your own reactivity unconditionally rewires you to love others' reactivity unconditionally too. Not so you don't do anything about it. You do something about it from the aspect of you that can create change. Your inherent transformer inside, your Essence.

Unconditional Love Awareness Generator

Read each statement and look inward to complete it.

One way I could bring unconditional love to my powerlessness each time it emerges is by ____.
(e.g., reminding myself unconditional love is what my powerlessness didn't get in the first place; bringing any Essence quality, because each Essence quality has unconditional love built into it; recognizing that I'm learning to trust that my softer side is powerful enough to create change easily)

One way I can be unconditionally loving toward my defensive strategies is by ____.
(e.g., practicing meeting what I've been trained to judge as good or bad, right or wrong, as stuckness in need of being valued; being playful and affectionate toward my Hero Pleaser, because it doesn't know how to take internal actions until I teach it; reminding myself that love transcends rightness or wrongness by seeing through it and tending to the need wishing to be met; recognizing my Villain as my trained-in Punisher of harms from the past [Villain Punishers are absolutely required in the right-or-wrong system—we all need a way to transact

for power within the right-or-wrong system, but not so much in the Essence system]; validating my Villain as being passed down through so many different humans in my family of origin [it's always been trying to help and doing great damage in its helping—I get to break this legacy of harm in relationships]; learning to love an aspect of me that I have been ashamed and afraid of).

Take a Moment to Choose this Moment

To bring unconditional love to your insides, you relinquish evaluations as the way to get better. They are too dysregulating. Dysregulation prevents transformation. You are teaching yourself to trust unconditional love as the way to transform anything into what you want it to be, especially your insides. Unconditional love trusts there is inherent goodness (Essence qualities) inside of you and each of us, while conditional love requires an external right-or-wrong system. Feel the settling internally as you reflect on your inherent goodness to be unconditionally loved.

Validating Your Trained-In Experience

Validation: "Yes, we were trained to believe that love is conditional and depends on how we behave."

Notice how your body responds. Any openness? Tightness? Both? You are rewiring emotional, nervous, attentional, hormonal, immune, and self-perception systems. Even noticing your body's response is a powerful internal action that regulates your feelings.

We were all taught to treat our insides the same way we were treated as kids. Speak this *Simple Truth*: "I'm now understanding how I've treated you, little ones, with conditional love in the same ways we were trained."

Notice how your body responds. Openings can emerge at the same time as the inner body recoils from feeling the shift in the status quo. Realizations can shock the system in a good way, but are so different from the usual that they can feel disorienting as your sense of self adapts. Your connection to your compassionate observing awareness inside gives you a safe place to watch the transformations happen in just the right timing your insides need.

If you feel unpleasant sensations, say: "I appreciate you, [insert sensation], for letting us know there's a need inside." Remind yourself that you are not the body sensation; you are the observing awareness attuning to it. Your present moment self is the "I" in this Simple Truth and the "us" is your past versions of you.

Say another *Simple Truth*: "I misunderstood your cries for help (powerlessness beliefs) as the truth about us."

Watch how your body responds. What does being understood in your body feel like? Notice the letting-go within the body. Tension releases, and lightness fills the vacancy. You are interrupting very entrenched patterns. That durable backpack of Simple Truths you carry now includes unconditional love.

Feel yourself giving unconditional love to the little past versions of you. You might even see their faces light up.

Validating Truth: "The truth about us is our unconditionally loving presence is required for change to happen."

Notice your body's response. You're reminding the little ones inside that they've always had this power to transform. They were always worthy of unconditional love. Your presence and your unconditional love sourced from Essence are your most powerful internal resources. They are the wellspring of growth, healing, and transformation.

Unconditional love transforms stuckness within and without by bringing Essence where Essence is absent. To trust the transformative power of unconditional love, we are required to see the Essence in each other, for each other, when it is temporarily absent. Our defensive strategies have pickled in a jar full of punishment as the catalyst for change. Someone doesn't act from Essence, and we punish them to get them back in Essence. This is forced change that emanates from fear, and so is not sustainable compared to change that emerges from Essence. Punish non-Essence to get a defensive strategy. Validate Essence to get Essence.

CHAPTER 14

The Essencey State of Safety

"A psychologically body-felt experience of safety is a primary need to be able to relax your sense of self into life. There are two ways to feel safe from sense-of-self threats: endlessly trying to control what's happening inside and outside of you OR easefully connecting to the truth inside of you. One will wear you out in a self-perpetuated prison; the other will set you free."

—Joni L. Davis

> Previously, we discovered the transforming power of un-
> conditional love. Our Essence qualities unconditionally
> love, and our defensive strategies conditionally love.
> This chapter invites you to dwell more frequently in your
> "Essencey state"—the fertile ground for transformation.
> Who knew we needed to retrain the mind and body to
> feel safe inside?

Feeling safe in our bodies is a need that went unmet for many of us. Safety gets imprinted from being understood instead of evaluated. Defensive strategies evaluate. Essence understands. If this need went unmet in you, you would have a powerlessness belief about how to feel safe that is not the truth about safety. You will feel incapable of feeling safe within and incompetent about how to create safety for others without realizing it.

If you do try to make others feel safe because you didn't get that need met, check in with your Pleasers, Protectors, or Punishers. Your Pleaser might be trying to be safe by keeping others from getting upset (unsafe). Your Protector might try to keep you safe by avoiding putting you in situations where you are evaluated or convincing you that you don't care about evaluations. Your Punisher will be busy evaluating the heck out of others before they can evaluate you. Once you step outside of these trained-in aspects of yourself and observe them, it explains a lot of the insane behaviors we all do while we're in them.

Safety means the absence of perceived threat to the sense of self. In a state of safety, our bodies are relaxed, and our minds are open to creativity. Humor arises more naturally. Sourcing safety from within means knowing how to regulate your emotional and nervous systems.

Most of us were trained to perceive safety externally, believing that we're safe when others are relaxed and unsafe when others are in defensive strategies. This leaves us dependent on other people's moods, behaviors, and reactions. It turns safety into a transaction, rather than an internally sourced truth.

Imagine having no ability to perceive threats to your sense of self. You wouldn't question your worth before trying something new. You wouldn't need external Validation. Instead, you'd feel safe being fully present, appreciating your Essence and that of others.

Take a Moment to Choose This Moment

If your safety depends on others, you're trapped in a cycle of going in and out of threat alert. Locate your safe place inside of you. Drop your wise and loving observing awareness into that space. Guide the parts of you that were trained to perceive threat back into regulation by soothing them with Simple Truths. From this place, others' defensive strategies no longer feel threatening—they feel like temporary states of disconnection and fear in others.

I was unconsciously taught that safety meant avoiding pain, not experiencing pleasure. I avoided emotional expression, difficult conversations, and others' pain. This training created limits I didn't even realize I had. I didn't feel satisfied because thriving didn't feel safe. I identified with avoiding pain, not experiencing joy. When I did thrive, my nervous system recoiled, as if thriving wasn't really me. I needed to retrain myself to feel safe while thriving and to feel safe inside instead of controlling things outside.

We've been trained to believe we are powerless to feel a body-felt sense of safety, especially when ignored or attacked.

Some related powerlessness beliefs are:

- *It's not safe to be fully me.*
- *My safety depends on how others treat me.*
- *I need to guard myself to protect my sense of self.*
- *Safety comes from doing everything right.*
- *I only feel safe within limitations.*

Body sensations like heaviness, queasiness, dissociation, and tightness are imprinted in our nervous systems as signs of unworthiness danger. These sensations become synonymous with helplessness, lostness, lovelessness, and unlovability.

To escape this despair, we stack defensive strategies on top of our body's real-time experience. But this bypasses the truth of the moment and blocks transformation. Safety isn't about bypassing feelings. It's about validating and being with them so they can transform.

By breaking the connection between difficult emotions (sadness, fear, anger) and powerlessness, you allow those emotions to fulfill their healthy roles:

- Sadness helps us process loss.
- Fear shows us what's missing.
- Anger helps us set boundaries.

Once you remove the direct link between these feelings and powerlessness, these emotions are no longer perceived as threats, and you can feel safe while feeling them.

Take a Moment to Choose This Moment

Reflect on the defensive strategies passed down to you.
Were they attempts to pseudo-regulate your emotional
and nervous systems into safety? Can you begin letting
go of the need to transact with the external world to
feel safe? Imagine: What would it feel like to no longer
depend on external circumstances for your inner peace,
to relax into being fully you, regardless of the world
around you?

Safety Awareness Generator

Complete the following reflections:

One way I was trained to source safety outside of myself is by ______

____.
(e.g., needing others to be happy and not upset with me; looking for
the right answer outside of myself; trusting my people-pleaser more
than my Essence; not making any mistakes; limiting my thriving)

One way my caretakers sourced safety outside of themselves was by

____.
(e.g., demanding others do what they wanted; controlling everyone's
experience; convincing themselves of their own justifications for their
behavior; following the rules; treating themselves as if the rules didn't
apply to them)

One way I can teach myself the skill of sourcing safety within is by

____.

(e.g., sourcing safety within my internal truth system; getting clear about what my powerlessness beliefs are and transforming them into Essence so I no longer perceive threats to my sense of self; putting a note up where I can see it: "Safety is a settled emotional and nervous system inside, not others' reactions")

One way I can interrupt the pattern of outsourcing my safety is _____

____.

(e.g., when my attention gets pulled into trying-to-be-right mode, I can pause and notice if I'm Essence breathing; catching my ruminating Protector going over and over the scenario in my head; by bringing Essence to my Pleaser, Protector, and Punisher so they can be exposed to Essencey inner options; by validating my powerlessness beliefs about safety and noticing how my body responds, then speaking a Validating Truth and noticing how my body responds)

Validating Your Trained-In Experience

Validation: "Yes, we were trained to believe our Essence could be wrong, so we are never safe from threat."

Notice how your body responds. Some parts may relax. Others may tighten. Especially notice your inner chest and gut areas. Notice any calming or grounding that allows you to sense you belong right where you are. Remind yourself: You are not your body sensations. Your body is offering information, not identity.

Speak this *Simple Truth*: "I'm putting together that we've misidentified our body sensations as the whole truth about who we are."

Notice how your body responds to being liberated from outside dependency and inside confusion. When you shift from identification to observation, Validation flows more easily.

Say this aloud: "This was the training we received, not the truth about us."

Notice what happens. This realization might stir strong sadness sensations. Let it be okay to be sad. Your observing awareness knows it's temporary and you won't get stuck in it. You are integrating something powerful.

Validating Truth: "The truth about us is our Essence experience of safety is measured by internal truth, not external judgments of right or wrong."

Notice how your body responds. You may feel tightness, sadness, joy, or openness. Whatever emerges, notice how good it feels to complete the loop by listening to your body and discerning truth from training.

Your safety is worthy of another round of Validations.

Validation: "Yes, we were trained to believe turning our attention inward is unsafe."

That's where all those icky feelings live, right? We're learning differently. Notice your body. Is there tightness? Openness? A desire to move? If so, gently follow the impulse.

Speak this *Simple Truth*: "I'm realizing some of our wires were crossed. Sometimes safety feels like tightness, and openness feels dangerous."

Let your body respond. You might feel sadness or fear as you realize you were trained to believe being guarded was the same as being safe.

Validating Truth: "The truth about us is our sense of self exists safely as inherent truth within us."

Notice how your body responds. If there is tightness, speak this to it: "I appreciate you, tightness, for letting us know how afraid we are of being wrong."

Observe what shifts inside. Bring loving, curious attention to the sensations. This is safety. This is internal truth. This is you returning to yourself.

Feeling free of causing or experiencing hurt, disappointment, rejection, or abandonment is an experience we all long to have. Unfortunately, these are the experiences that our defensive strategies are trying to get each other to take responsibility for through endless power struggles. Psychological safety requires each of us to take responsibility for our own powerlessness fears of being disappointed, rejected, or abandoned. Psychological safety means perceiving no threat to the sense of self. The sense of self is not powerless to feel worthy or lovable when it feels validated.

To clarify, the safety we're talking about doesn't mean there isn't a potential threat to the sense of self—for example, someone's Punisher attacking your character. Safety means you no longer perceive anything as a threat to your sense of self: "Their defensive strategies have nothing to do with our worthiness." Notice how your body is learning to perceive truth as the new safety. You've validated your powerlessness back into power, so you no longer feel unworthy, and this transforms how you perceive threat. You remind yourself it's their defensive strategies and not their Essence that attacks. Their defensive strategies can't see the truth about you. Their Essence can. Feeling safe internally is real freedom. Validate to locate your safety inside.

CHAPTER 15

Receiving

"Until we can receive with an open heart, we're never really giving with an open heart. When we attach judgment to receiving help, we knowingly or unknowingly attach judgment to giving help."

—Brené Brown

Previously, we learned to access and sustain your Essencey state by sourcing safety from within. We explored how our bodies regulate when we're perceiving ourselves outside of the right-or-wrong system and embedded in inner truth. Now, we'll discover how identity—yes, identity—is shaped around receiving and how you can evolve your receiving skills from fear-based survival into conscious creation.

Feeling empowered and worthy when receiving so that receiving and giving are balanced is a need that went unmet for many of us. If this need went unmet in you, you would feel powerless about being worthy of receiving Validation or comfort and soothing and not be adept at validating, comforting, or soothing others because it wasn't modeled for you. This can transform.

Start the transformation by noticing your Pleasers, Protectors, and Punishers. Your Pleaser may feel like it has failed if you try to receive. It's trained to be the giver, not the receiver. Your Protector might fire off a diatribe in your head about how you'll owe someone something if you receive. (Not true but convincing when it is happening.) And your Punisher may bully you or somebody else for being needy!

Receiving means being able to accept comfort and care without feeling guilty, like we owe someone or we're wrong or bad for needing it. It means allowing ourselves to take in what is offered by others, so they, too, can balance their giving and receiving. When we truly receive within self-generated grace and dignity, our mind and body feel known and loved. We no longer feel the need to diminish or forsake our needs; we feel worthy of being supported.

We can receive love, gifts, good news, bad news, attention, and feedback all in presence and wholeness. To truly receive, we are required to notice how our body responds to what has been given or what is happening. Internal *presence* is required to receive external *presents*. The act of noticing your internal state from your compassionate observing awareness is you giving to the parts of you that didn't learn to receive. Your observing awareness has the resources and awareness to cultivate calmness and balance inside right while you're having an experience that doesn't feel calm or balanced at all. Your observing awareness rewires your insides every time you tap into it.

Take a Moment to Choose This Moment

When feeling vulnerable or uncomfortable receiving,
do you slip into a quick defensive strategy to escape
the moment? Notice what habitual maneuvering you
do. Can you challenge yourself to interrupt this old,
stuck pattern by shifting your internal state from vulnerability back into your pure authenticity? As soon as you
validate the vulnerability, it melts into your authenticity.
You shift from un-present to receive the present right
back into presence. When you let yourself receive, you
feel the power and love of the connection between the
giver and the receiver.

We've all been trained how to receive, and for most of us, it's through a defensive strategy, usually some sort of deflection. You can teach yourself how to receive from your Essence instead. One clear way to explore this is by noticing how you receive positive and negative feedback. When we're in a guarded state, we struggle to receive. We might think we don't deserve it, or we might start telling ourselves stories like *They feel sorry for me because I'm less than.* We want to teach ourselves to receive from Essence so we can be touched by others' authenticity.

Receiving is enhanced by giving savoring attention to your body as you receive.

Take a Moment to Choose This Moment

Sit back and recall the last few times you were given
compliments or appreciation. How did you receive this?
Did you look the other person in the eye and let them fully
in? Or did you deflect in some way? Now think of the last
time you were given feedback you interpreted as negative. How did you receive that? Did you let it in without
making yourself right or wrong? Were you able to process
it without getting defensive externally or in your head?

Most of us learned to receive through the filters of right or wrong.
Our own right-or-wrong listening filter can perceive someone making
us wrong when they are speaking the truth to us. We ask ourselves
some version of *Am I worthy enough to receive this?* Or demand *I don't
deserve to be attacked this way.* No matter how our defensive strategies
answer, we're still playing the very sticky right-or-wrong game.

Receiving is a vulnerable moment, and most of us have been
trained to avoid vulnerability. It can make us feel self-conscious and
wordlessly floundering, which can diminish our experience of joy in
receiving. But wouldn't it be great to teach yourself to feel joy in receiving by transforming any vulnerability to receiving?

Common powerlessness beliefs related to receiving include:

- *If I am open to receiving, I am open to being hurt.*
- *It's selfish to receive.*
- *If I receive, it's too painful when it goes away.*
- *If I am my behavior, then receiving feedback about my behavior
  is a threat to my sense of self.*
- *Receiving makes me feel vulnerable, and I hate that feeling.*

Take a Moment to Choose This Moment

Write down your negative beliefs about receiving.
Writing puts us into observing awareness, allowing us
to learn more than we can from within a fear-based
mindset. Taking time to reflect and write tells your inner
self that you are worthy of this time and attention. This
helps you feel worthy of receiving.

I had so many emotional needs unmet in childhood, even though I came from a good family. This training made me super-needy while acting like I wasn't. I would pull people in, then push them away. I'd form deep connections and then ghost people, scared and unaware of it. I idealized partners and friends, trying to get them to be someone they weren't. All of this was rooted in fear. Looking back, I now see I was unavailable to receive emotional care. I couldn't receive what others were giving because I was too busy trying to get something else from them. *Duh, it's me. I'm the problem, it's me!* I needed to learn how to feel worthy of having my needs met so that my defensive strategies didn't block my ability to receive.

It's almost impossible to receive and express at the same time. Most of us were trained to feel incompetent if we couldn't find the right words in the moment. Often, we talk without checking in with how our words land with ourselves or others. To truly receive, we need to pause that pesky autopilot and be present with our internal experience. This means stepping into observing awareness even while feeling awkward or extremely uncomfortable.

A big reason we struggle with receiving is that we were never taught the value of noticing how our body responds. We also weren't taught how to be with and transform uncomfortable sensations. Most of us were taught to say, "Thank you" without checking in with our internal experience. We rushed to take the appropriate external action, cutting ourselves off from our internal truth and a potent moment of truly connecting with another. We learned to protect ourselves from receiving to avoid the uncomfortable sensations of powerlessness.

Receiving is where powerlessness started for most of us. We were trained to be extraordinarily uncomfortable with it, not because receiving itself is painful, but because of the right-or-wrong system. Growing up, every time we received feedback from others' defensive strategies, it imprinted unworthiness. That unworthiness erupts as discomfort when someone tries to meet this need of worthiness in the present.

When we receive from someone's Essence to our Essence, it feels safe. But receiving from defensive strategies feels like a threat. If feedback comes from another's defensive strategy, it feels like you must change who you are to be accepted. In contrast, when it comes from Essence, you feel valued. Likewise, when you're in your own Essence, feedback you give yourself feels safe and affirming.

Receiving Awareness Generator

Reflect on each statement below and complete it with what arises for you:

Since our Hero people-pleaser keeps us from receiving by keeping us focused externally, one way I can build the skill of focusing internally is by ____.
(e.g., reminding myself it's safe to look within; reminding myself my powerlessness can be transformed—it's not something I have to try to avoid anymore; reminding myself that looking within settles my emotional and nervous systems, so I can trust myself to know truth and be free to receive; using the Simple Truth mantra: Hero Pleaser focuses without, Essence focuses within; realizing that even if my Hero

Pleaser is not taking any external actions, it's still trolling my internal thoughts about what happened externally.)

A way I can make friends with my uncomfortable body sensations is by ____.
(e.g., meeting my uncomfortable body sensations with some Essencey presence; getting curious about what powerlessness belief is causing my uncomfortable body sensations; locating myself internally as the observing awareness of my uncomfortableness, so I have some distance from and perspective on it instead of leaving my sense of self submerged with it)

One way I can disidentify my sense of self from my uncomfortableness in the moment of receiving is by _______________________________.
(e.g., speaking Simple Truths to my uncomfortableness; feeling compassion for my Pleaser's, Protector's, or Punisher's uncomfortableness; doing Essence breathing)

One way I can transform my uncomfortableness into power is by ___

____.
(e.g., owning it as training and not the truth about us; expressing that I'm uncomfortable AND I'm sexy; being loving toward the vulnerability I'm feeling so my vulnerability can relax and help me connect the dots about my training)

The repetitive phrases my Hero Pleaser and Villainy Punisher convince me are truth, and which keep me from receiving are _________

____.
(e.g., Hero Pleaser: *It was no big deal*; Hero Pleaser: *Don't make a fuss about it*; Hero Pleaser: *Anybody could have done it*; Villainy Punisher: *You never appreciated me before!*; Villainy Punisher: *You didn't give me any choice!*; Villainy Punisher: *You have no idea what I sacrificed!*; Villainy Punisher: *That's it?! That's all I get? A thank-you? I gave up everything for you!*)

Validating Your Trained-In Experience Around Receiving

Validation: "Yes, we were trained to believe receiving opens us to threats to our sense of self. (So, it felt easier to stay closed.)"

Notice how your body responds. Every time you notice your body's response, you are practicing receiving.

You might feel sadness recognizing how little you've been able to receive as an enjoyable body-felt experience. Speak this *Simple Truth* to your sadness: "I know sadness allows us to let go of what wasn't working." Notice your body's response. Appreciate yourself for learning to receive by valuing your internal experience.

For any tightness in your body, try this: "I'm realizing receiving often felt like a threat to our sense of self." Notice what unfolds.

Another *Simple Truth*: "Receiving what others give us by trying it on within our body requires reconnecting with our body." Notice your body as it tries on receiving.

And one more: "I'm noticing our fear of feeling powerlessness has kept us from receiving goodness too." Notice any place inside that lets go into relaxation when it hears the truth.

Validating Truth: "The truth about us is we can transform our inner powerlessness into our inner goodness, making it safe to receive goodness."

Notice how your body responds. Let yourself feel without judgment.

Final *Simple Truth*: "Disidentifying our sense of self from body sensations allows us to amplify pleasant ones and transform unpleasant ones."

Notice how your body receives what is given.

The major reason most of us have trouble receiving is because we were not exposed to the value of noticing how our body responds to what's happening. Most of us were instead trained to be our Heroing Pleaser. Our Pleasers are supposed to give and not receive. Pleasers often feel like failures if they need to receive.

Unfortunately for all of us, our Heroing Pleaser defensive strategies distract us from how our body is responding to what's happening.
Without this mind/body connection, the pathway to Essence is cut off.
Our Heroing Pleaser's primary role is to distract us from the powerlessness that already resides inside of us. It does this by cutting off the
brain's connections to what the body is experiencing. Memory alert:
Remember how the right prefrontal cortex can go offline and sever
the mind's experience of the body. To gain trust in using this pathway
again, you can now see how you need some trust in the ability of your
observing awareness to transform powerlessness so that you no longer
identify as your powerlessness.

The uncomfortableness you feel in your body when receiving appreciations of genuine human connection is your Heroing Pleaser not
knowing what to do with what it has worked so hard to secure. As
soon as you know you are the one who's aware of their uncomfortableness, you are no longer fused with it and can transform it. Who knew?!
Our uncomfortableness just needed some comforting to transform it.
Validate to strengthen your receiving pathways.

You are growing the capacity to receive. From here, the balance
of giving and receiving becomes a flow, not a transaction. Validate to
regulate your uncomfortableness around receiving.

CHAPTER 16

Creativity

"The meaning I picked, the one that changed my life:
Overcome fear, behold wonder."

—Richard Bach

Previously, we explored how identity evolves from
Essence when needs are met or devolves into fear from
unmet needs. We explored how receiving is not only
something we forget to do but also something we unconsciously block. "Validate to regulate uncomfortableness" became our mantra. This next chapter is where
the rubber meets the road—integrating all your learning
into your moment-to-moment originality.

Creativity is creating something from nothing. Moment-to-moment creativity is being so present in your experience that something new emerges from within you, guiding, resolving, or surprising you in real time. It can be playful or powerful. It's your mind and body working together in the now to let something novel arise. Unfortunately, this need often goes unmet in childhood, as fear thwarts creativity.

If this need went unmet in you, you would feel powerless about your ability to spontaneously tap into new ideas within. You will also have trouble identifying and validating other people's moment-to-moment creativity. If you can appreciate others' creativity, check to see whether it's a Pleaser, Protector, or Punisher who might desperately need appreciation in return. If you can appreciate another's creativity without needing anything in return, it's authentic. If you can use other people's amazing ideas as the springboard to come up with your own, you're in Essence.

Your Pleaser doesn't know how to do this. It's too busy trying to survive by striving and efforting to be good and by keeping others seeing you as good to have the time to generate new and fresh ideas in the moment. Your Protector might pretend others' ideas are your own so people see you as amazing. Your Punisher might diminish others' creativity so you don't feel bad about not having your own. Observe through your expanding awareness these various voices in your head and cultivate an Essencey voice that speaks Simple Truths to these aspects of you. They have authenticity in them; it's just been untrusted.

Your life is your art, what you are experiencing, expressing, and producing from Essence. Moment-to-moment creativity lives where your mind attunes to your body's internal state, allowing a stream of spontaneous, insightful responses. It helps you see through what's happening rather than being swept up in it.

For example, instead of autoreacting with *Stop yelling at me!* when someone erupts in anger, you can drop into your inner creativity and recognize their defensive strategy as fear. This opens space to respond with something like *I can tell this really matters to you and you want to know it matters to me.*

Your moment-to-moment creativity is vital to feeling satisfaction, fulfillment, and meaning even during challenges. When you're internally regulated, your creativity becomes a source of joy. If you surprise yourself with a new idea, it feels meaningful because it reflects your Essence qualities.

Take a Moment to Choose This Moment

When do you feel your moment-to-moment creativity? Fear and defensive strategies block this connection because they pull you into the past or the future. Let your compassionate observing awareness settle your alert system so you can drop into your body and the present moment. *Simple Truth:* "I'm realizing our automatic powerlessness fears have been shifting us out of the present moment where our ever-evolving creativity lives." Notice your you-know-what.

Creativity helps you move from co-complaining to co-creating. Complaining tries to validate your suffering by making you right and others wrong. Creating validates your presence by contributing something new. When you're not feeling fulfilled, ask: "What Essence quality am I craving to express or experience?"

Your moment-to-moment creativity makes you unique. It emerges from wonder and curiosity.

Take a Moment to Choose This Moment

Wonder about your uniqueness. Be curious about
how your perspective changes the world. Wonder
about your defensive strategies and how they've been
trying—unsuccessfully—to get the world to recognize
your uniqueness. Appreciate the creativity already within you that wants to live.

The angle from which you choose to view a situation, the words
you choose to speak, and the Essence qualities you express combine
into an irreproducible moment of being you that no one else can repli-
cate. This is your gift to the world.

I used to regurgitate other people's creative ideas and claim them
as my own because I didn't think I had anything meaningful to offer
from my own insides. I longed to feel that my voice mattered. It wasn't
anyone's fault; it was just the training I received. When I realized I
wasn't lacking, but rather was untrained in accessing my creativity, I
cried for everyone who hadn't been taught they had something meaningful inside to express. Now, I use other people's creativity as a rocket
ship to come up with my own ideas from the inspiration of their ideas.
I marinate in their ideas until my own creative thoughts emerge from
deep within.

We've been trained not to trust that creativity will emerge from
within us.

Common powerlessness beliefs are:

- *I am not creative.*
- *I can't come up with my own ideas.*
- *I'm not talented. Creativity is for the gifted.*

- *There's nothing inside me worthy of expressing.*
- *I have nothing of value to offer.*

Creativity isn't just artistic performance. It's how you answer, "How are you?" It's in how you say, "I love you." Creativity can be found in every Simple Truth you choose to express, each time slightly differently, and soooo authentically.

Some More Simple Truths About Creativity

- Moment-to-moment creativity is emergent. It flows whether or not you notice.
- It's only accessible when your mind is valuing your internal body experience.
- Seeing through what's happening, instead of suffering from it, expands creativity.
- Curiosity and moment-to-moment creativity are partners.
- Your creativity shapes your external actions. When connected internally, you don't need to prove or conceal—you simply express.

Creativity Awareness Generators

One way I can notice when I'm in defensive mode and not creative mode is by ____.
(e.g., noticing if I'm automatically trying to be right about something, even little things, like directions or logistics [it's still reactivity]; reflecting on my caretakers' defensive strategies because I am unconsciously doing them until I catch myself; remembering I have deeper and broader infinite solutions on the other side of me [the Essence side])

One way I can transform my reactivity into creativity is by _________

____.

(e.g., validating my trained-in powerlessness; validating to regulate; noticing my body sensations; invoking an Essence quality; speaking a Simple Truth to myself)

One Essence quality I want to bring forward is _______________________. (Not-so-subtle hint: Practice them all until they are integrated into your Unconscious Procedural Manual. There's not a bad option in the bunch.)

One way I can trust my creativity in adversity is by _______________. (e.g., speaking a *Simple Truth* when I'm powerless: "We were trained to feel powerless and not creative when we're up Schitt's Creek" [then notice my inner body—the playfulness reminds me of my Essence in the moment]; bringing my moment-to-moment creativity right to my reactivity by imagining what need my reactivity is trying to get met for me, such as unconditional love, the mind/body connection, or trusting my choices; focusing on the results I want to create instead of the wrongs that are being committed)

When I'm in my moment-to-moment creativity, my body feels _______
____.
(e.g., expanded; in the flow; powerful; satisfied; fulfilled)

Validating Your Trained-In Experience Around Creativity

Validation: "Yes, most of us were taught that creativity only counts if it brings money or recognition."

Notice how your body responds. Does your body open with truth, or contract in resistance? Either is valuable information. Speak this *Simple Truth*: "I'm realizing we saw our talents as external achievements, not internal resources." Linger here, outside your feelings as the feelings arise.

Another *Simple Truth*: "I'm learning how to explore my feelings and limitations without making anything wrong." Let this wash through your body.

Validating Truth: "The truth about us is we are unique for how we experience, express, and create from Essence."

Notice how your body responds. This is the return to noticing and celebrating your inner brilliance. Yes, it's always been inside of you, sometimes blocked by fear.

You have something inside of you that is so valuable! Your unique and unmatched ability to create something from nothing, moment to moment. Validating the fears you imprinted in your youth, about whether you had anything in there that was worthy of contributing, dissolves the fears and drops you smack-dab into your creative self. If you aren't creating in this moment, you're reacting. Validate to create.

CHAPTER 17

Trusting from Within

"If you must look back, do so forgivingly. If you will
look forward, do so prayerfully. But the wisest course
would be to be present in the present gratefully."

—Maya Angelou

"The glue that holds all relationships together—
including the relationship between the leader and
the led—is trust, and trust is based on integrity."

—Brian Tracy

"When people honor each other, there is a trust
established that leads to synergy, interdependence,
and deep respect. Both parties make decisions and
choices based on what is right, what is best, what is
valued most highly."

—Blaine Lee

Previously, we were integrating your learning into your special gift to yourself and the world, your moment-to-moment creativity. You're one of eight billion, and no one does moment-to-moment creativity like you do. Life and you are boring without it. (Giggle.) Here you'll focus on how to transform emotional overwhelm into regulation, using Essence as your inner anchor. Transforming overwhelm or confusion builds your trust muscles.

Trust is the ability to access what's true inside of you. It originates within and is always available when you are in a settled internal state, when your medial prefrontal cortex is online and you're attuned to your body in the moment. We trust integrity, which means doing what you say you will do and not doing what you say you won't do. Trust is a core need that goes unmet in many of us. If this need was unmet in you, you will feel powerless about trusting yourself or others. Your Pleasers, Protectors, and Punishers will have all kinds of powerlessness beliefs about trust running their intentions.

Your Pleaser will have been trained to overtrust and get burned. Your Protector might undertrust and miss out on being able to get really close to another in relationship. Your Punisher will be spouting stories about how not trusting is safer than trusting. These aspects of you are desperately trying to get your needs met without knowing how to trust your Essence to do it.

We learn to trust ourselves by doing what we say we will do and not doing what we say we won't, especially in private commitments we make to ourselves. When we follow through on exercise, nourishment, hard conversations, or rest, even when no one is watching, we build self-trust through integrity and consistency.

Your people-pleaser self often wants the easier route. Your trained-in powerlessness and defensive strategies are the two forces most likely to knock you out of self-trust. But when you trust your own integrity, you'll recognize others who do the same or set boundaries with those who can't. You can't trust others when you're in defensive mode. Only from Essence can you access the truth inside and discern the same in others.

Trusting others begins with trusting yourself. When you can discern whether someone is in their authenticity or acting from fear and defensiveness, your trust becomes clearer. You don't trust their defensive strategies; you trust their Essence. You can remain calm and centered by remembering their authenticity is still there, even if they can't access it in the moment. From this calmness, you can respond with Simple Truths that encourage self-reflection rather than defensiveness.

Operating from trust allows you to navigate the world from grounded, powerful emotional and nervous systems. You recognize that when you go into alert, it's usually a trust issue rooted in past experiences. Alert states bring either/or thinking and disconnect you from your Essence. When you can feel trust internally, you make sense of chaos and remain settled even while the world spins. You become a placeholder for equanimity, an anchor of sanity through Essence in turbulent times.

Take a Moment to Choose This Moment

Imagine a situation where you trust yourself. How does your body feel when you follow through on a challenging commitment? Trust and integrity often feel like bursts of energy and swirling satisfaction through your spine.
This imprint of internal reliability lives in your connective tissue as scaffolding. It's the structure you build internally to consistently show up for yourself.

Cynthia, a client of mine, didn't trust herself or others. Her powerful, skeptical Protector ruled her internal world, trained to believe no one could or would ever truly comfort her. Her people-pleaser persona helped others but didn't believe her needs would be met in return. She longed for closeness but pushed people away with her critical inner and then outer voice. Her skeptic labeled others as incompetent. Her people-pleaser kept her from trusting herself. Her needs couldn't be met because her defenses blocked the very experiences she craved. When others offered care, her incompetency-Punisher stepped in to invalidate it as not the right type of care.

Notice the paradox? Cynthia's inability to trust others made her untrustworthy to others. She would misjudge their actions as hostile when they were attempting to care for her. Her mistrust stemmed from the training her caregivers' defensive strategies required her to develop just to try to meet her need for trust. We validated her overreliance on pleasing, skepticism, resenting, and punishing, as well as her belief that trust was too dangerous. That Validation was the soothing she'd always needed. It opened her belief system to a new truth: She could teach herself how to trust.

We've been trained to believe that our Essence is powerless to receive comfort and soothing from others. That we can't trust them to care for us. We weren't taught we are worthy of comfort. Helplessness and hopelessness—deep branches of powerlessness—often begin here. Helplessness is not trusting anyone can soothe your pain. Hopelessness is believing nothing will ever change.

These originate in childhood when we felt rejected or unsupported by caretakers caught in their own defensive loops. It felt like death to our sense of self. We learned to distrust our feelings and believed no one cared. We stopped trusting our feelings and instead focused on trying to change others' behavior, hoping to earn care by being what our caregivers needed.

But knowing you can trust others when they are in Essence allows you to navigate trust skillfully. When others are open, flexible, and consistent, they are in Essence and safe to trust. When closed, rigid, or inconsistent, they are reactive. You don't take it personally. You trust your capacity to stay grounded, to respond with Essence, and to transform environments where Essence can emerge.

Some powerlessness beliefs that keep us from trusting include:

- *If I need comfort, I'm weak. I can't trust myself.*
- *No one will ever know how to comfort me.*
- *I'm not worthy of comfort, so I can't trust it.*
- *No one will help when I need it. I can't trust that anyone cares.*
- *Others always ruin my good feelings. I can't trust my own joy.*

Trust Awareness Generator

How I can recognize that I distrust my Essence when others are doing the same is by ____.
(e.g., feeling my nervous system revving up or shutting down; noticing my breathing becoming guarded and shallow; noticing my familiar repeating patterns [such as, when others withdraw, I get anxious about my wrongness, or, when they raise their voice, I top their fighty anger with my own])

One way I can create nervous system trust in all my interactions is by ____.
(e.g., settling my own nervous system threat alert mode first; getting very familiar with the internal needs that I'm trying to get met with a dysregulated nervous system, so I can speak Simple Truths to them to regulate my nervous system; sensing the body signals of dysregulation in myself and others [internal issue], so I can know when it's time to speak Simple Truths and when it's time to actively resolve the outer issue [Hint: Speak Simple Truths before you try to resolve anything])

One way I can increase trust in myself when I or others are perceiving a threat is by ____.

(e.g., noticing the right-or-wrong system we just stepped in; familiar-
izing myself with how I've been trained to unconsciously make myself
and others wrong with hidden defensive strategies; grounding myself
in the truth [reminding myself that humans only get defensive when
they are perceiving a threat to their sense of self as being wrong: failing, unwanted, unloved, unworthy])

One way I can trust my power to transform interactions is by _______
____.

(e.g., mastering speaking Simple Truths [it's such an exquisite power
when you feel them emerge from deep inside you]; taking a moment
to notice how powerful it feels to have a relationship with your insides
that is rich with aliveness and discovery because you have faced your
internal fears; practice, practice, practice [it's a skill you can develop,
and even though it takes some practice, you could learn to enjoy the
process])

Validating Your Trained-In Experience Around Trust

When parents attune to their children's inner experiences, they imprint trust: "There is abundance within us. We don't need to fear its
loss or lack." This inner trust of abundant resources inside you is the
antidote to abandonment fears and other sense-of-self threats.

Validation: "Yes, we were trained to believe that trusting others means
trusting their perception of our worth in that moment."

Notice how your body responds. Do you feel a settling or a tightening? Let your body distill your experience. Listen inwardly. Memories might emerge.

Speak this *Simple Truth*: "I'm realizing where we locate our sense
of self—Essence or Stack—impacts our ability to trust." Notice what
shifts. When you observe from within, you can feel the moment trust
turns back on.

Another *Simple Truth*: "Our worthiness of having our needs met is not dependent on whether someone else is in Essence." Notice the internal shifts. Repeat it a few times. Let your system try it on.

Validating Truth: "The truth about us is our internal discernment houses our sense of self in truth, creating trust."

Notice how your body responds to being valued by your mind. Your mind experiences life through your body's sensations. If you're not noticing them, you're not having the full experience.

Speak this *Simple Truth*: "I'm realizing how important our body sensations are to knowing truth and building trust." Notice what happens.

Another *Simple Truth*: "We learned to cut off trust in our body's signals to avoid feeling powerlessness." Feel what comes. Remember, your head also has sensations. If it feels marshmallowy, you're integrating. If it feels fuzzy and you can't think, you may be dissociating. Speak to it with compassion: "Thank you, dissociation, for letting us know there's fear that needs attention." Notice how your system responds. Dissociation transforms back into presence when met with Essence, better known as truth.

It's impossible to trust others unless you're in your Essence qualities. When you are in your Essence qualities, you can access what's true inside of you. You can remember that when others aren't in their Essence qualities, it's only momentary; it's not forever. You're also aware of your capacity to interact with another's Essence qualities, especially when they're in their defensive strategies. You are trusting your ability to transform interactions by originating from your Essence. Whichever aspect of them you communicate with, you will receive communication from that aspect of them in return.

You don't HAVE to do this, and you know it. You choose to do it when your intuitions and instincts let you know it's what you want. You choose to bring Essence to an interaction when you sense an opening to do so. Conveying you can be trusted by emanating Essence creates contexts, environments, settings, and conditions that broadcast nervous system safety for all, allows everyone to drop their need for defenses, and invites Essence qualities forward, engendering trust.

Self-trust is about knowing what's true for you, especially when your powerlessness, Pleaser, Protector, or Punisher voices are attempting to convince you there is a threat to your sense of self. You cannot trust yourself to stay true to your Essence intentions whenever your physiology is in a state of perceiving threats to the self.

For example, if you're in a state of proving someone else is wrong about you, you cannot trust that your self is grounded in your Essence. Essence doesn't do the endless who's-right-who's-wrong thing. Trusting yourself to follow through with your stated intentions requires you to be rooted in your Essence. Your intention is to validate to regulate, not defend yourself against untruths. If you validate, they will take ownership of their untruths, and you don't have to work so hard to get them to see them.

You are learning to trust again. From within. Validate to trust.

CHAPTER 18

Autonomy and Connection

"You mustn't confuse a single failure with a final defeat."

—F. Scott Fitzgerald

Previously, we learned how to emotionally regulate and integrate trust in your Essence. Healing the fears from the past that caused your self-doubt by noticing what's stuck in your nervous system that's not supposed to be there. This chapter explores how autonomy can coexist with connection—and how it can become a source of empowered choice.

Autonomy is the feeling of freedom and competence to explore unknowns while staying connected to your Essence qualities, your internal resources. It's the knowing that you have what it takes inside to handle anything that comes your way. Autonomy means you feel the presence of your internal resources, making it safe to seek and explore new experiences. As a child, you needed to be able to look back and see your caretaker's reassurance that you were safe and capable when you went exploring. Defensive strategies aren't good at conveying capability in others; they're too busy trying to feel capable themselves.

Autonomy is a need that went unmet for many of us. If the need for autonomy went unmet in you, you will have powerlessness imprinted in your Unconscious Procedural Manual about your agency to face unknowns and help others face unknowns. Your Pleaser might give up your autonomy as the only way to belong and stay connected. Your Protector might have a debate with you in your head that being in connection takes your autonomy away. Your Punisher may criticize you for wanting to feel your agency to explore and discover novelty because you'll outgrow your needed community.

Connection—emotional connection—is a need that went unmet for almost all of us also. If the need for emotional connection went unmet in you, you will feel powerlessness about being able to emotionally connect with yourself and therefore others. Your Pleaser may idealize others, hoping to get the connection you never got in childhood. Your Protector may diminish connection to feel your agency to do what you want. And your Punisher may be incessantly monitoring others' behavior and how it isn't giving you the connection you need.

In order to emotionally connect with yourself and others, you need to know how to validate feelings—something most of us were not taught to do. Our trained-in powerlessness and the Pleaser, Protector, and Punisher defensive strategies we auto-run to turn the power back on all disconnect us from our inner selves and others' inner worlds. Most of us are emotionally dehydrated by our longing for connection and our inability to drink it in when it's available.

Autonomy means being able to explore unknowns without fearing that your sense of self is under threat. The secret to feeling autonomous isn't never feeling fear; it's knowing what to do with fear when it shows up. Autonomy is about transforming moments of stuckness by validating your fears and learning to regulate them. We weren't taught how to regulate fear. We were taught to be swept away by it. Fears need comforting and soothing to settle: *It's okay we're afraid, we've never done this before.* Notice how your body responds when you give it this type of attention. You become the one who reassures yourself. You're self-directing your internal experience and feeling free to make choices that feel intuitively right for you.

Connection is about feeling free to be completely you while emotionally connecting to another. Emotional connections satisfy many of our other needs like empathy and understanding, trust, deep communication, support, shared experiences, and respect. Most people I talk to think they can emotionally connect because they can feel. They don't realize what habitually gets in the way of their feelings and therefore their availability for connection.

When we operate from autonomy, we trust our moral independence. Our inner guidance is sourced from our core values, which are Essence qualities like integrity, compassion, and kindness. From Essence, you'll find your autonomy can work with, not against, others' needs for autonomy and connection.

When emotionally connected to ourselves by connecting our mind and body through Validations and body attunement, we trust our ability to connect with others. Emotionally connecting with ourselves requires our mind to check in with our body's sensations and notice what we are feeling moment to moment. This simple but profound internal action shifts us instantly from thinking and talking about our feelings to thinking from and expressing from our feelings. This underestimated inner action adds flavor and enriches our experience, making life—and us—more attractive. It's why you can listen to some people all day long, but you would be willing to sell your ears when listening to others.

Our minds and bodies relax, and we co-create experiences with others free from any threat to our sense of self, our autonomy, and our connection.

Take a Moment to Choose This Moment

Reflect on your self-governing. How do trust, autonomy, and integrity show up in how you treat yourself? Were you taught that it's safe to explore? Or were you trained to need certainty before trying anything? Explore how your Pleaser, Protector, and Punisher govern and organize your insides. Notice how powerlessness beliefs may have become your self-governing strategies instead of your Essence. Teach your defensive strategies how to trust their own autonomy by guiding them out of either/or thinking and into both/and. Speak this *Simple Truth*: "I'm realizing that as an adult, no one can take away our autonomy—except our own defenses and powerlessness." Notice how your body responds.

I once believed autonomy and connection were mutually exclusive. To me, being self-governing felt selfish. So, I justified what I wanted when no one else was looking, eating things alone that I wouldn't eat around others, flirting outside my relationships. I thought relationships had rules I had to escape from to feel free. I didn't know I could feel empowered and self-governed and still emotionally connect. I needed to learn to set internal boundaries that felt good, instead of sneaking around with pseudo-autonomy. In reflection, a memory surfaced of my dad modeling the belief "If no one else saw it, it didn't happen." That belief shaped me more than I was aware. But if I learned it, I could unlearn it. I can heal my past by transforming in my present. I can learn what authentic autonomy and connection truly are.

We've been trained to believe we're powerless to experience ourselves as separate, unique creators—especially when we feel different from others. Often, we were taught to govern ourselves to be like someone else, not like ourselves (especially caretakers we were different from). But autonomy means feeling safe and powerful enough to explore unknowns.

Some common powerlessness beliefs around autonomy include:

- *Someone or something is trying to thwart me.*
- *I can't do it on my own.*
- *I can't be authentic and still be loved.*
- *It's not safe to explore new things.*
- *If I'm afraid, I'm doing it wrong.*
- *Feeling incompetently uncomfortable is a bad thing.*

We've also been taught that being in connection with others makes us feel vulnerable to losing that connection. Many of us unconsciously limit our ability to need others because we can't bear the insecurity of losing that person. Others of us were taught that we need other people to be able to know who we are. We can't tell who we are until we've seen it in someone else's eyes.

Some powerlessness beliefs about connection are:

- *I am how you see me. I need to maintain my connection with you to know who I am.*
- *Being in connection with others limits who I am.*
- *I have to give my power away to stay connected.*
- *I have to overpower others to get what I need in connection.*
- *Connections always disappoint me.*

When we're in defensive mode, we want others to think like us so we can get what we want while simultaneously wanting to be different and special. This creates a push-pull with our autonomy. We long to stand out, yet fear being judged for it. Like the aspiring influencer who delays posting due to fear.

Our sense of autonomy was formed in our Unconscious Procedural Manual by age five. Depending on that training, we now meet challenges from either our Essence or our defensive strategies. From Essence, autonomy looks like trying something new, observing the outcome, learning, and trying again until we get what we want.

When parents aren't in touch with their own Essence, they often build fear into their children's autonomy. Think of the fear-based belief "I'm not a good parent if __________." That fear pushes parents into defensive mode, teaching kids what not to do instead of what they can do. Even well-meant warnings like *Be careful* subtly train children to focus on what to avoid, not what to create. Maybe we could say to each other *Be Essencey* instead.

The secret to true agency in autonomy is balancing the need for connection with the need for independence. But to do that, we need to transform the fears we hold about both. Does connection feel safe or dangerous? What about autonomy? In relationships, one partner often feels safer in connection and the other in autonomy. Without awareness, these imprints become points of tension. Team Connection may see autonomy as abandonment. Team Autonomy may see connection as entrapment. These become attachment styles. Remember, this was trained into you. It's not who you really are or how things really are.

You can use your autonomy to study your connection/autonomy model. Were you taught to settle through connection or by getting away? Become the observing awareness of your beliefs and then of your body sensations. Your observing awareness is the place where your realizations emerge because it's where your balance lives.

For example, I had a client who felt deep shame whenever others were upset with her. That shame sent her fleeing into isolation. She believed herself to be independent, but it was a pseudo-autonomy—a Stacked reaction to protect her sense of self. Her powerlessness draining her of her aliveness while her Protector tried to turn the power back on by proving she didn't need others.

Another example is how our People-pleasers and Protectors knock us out of authentic connection because they knock us out of alignment with our postural experience of power in our bodies. Most of us jut our head forward in front of our spine when we are in Pleaser mode. Others of us pull our heads backward behind our usual spinal alignment when we auto-register into Protector mode. These postural misalignments unconsciously convey to others that we are not available for authentic connection. Invoking awareness about these postural shifts allows us to notice when we are disconnected from our inner alignment both physically and emotionally. Time to validate to align with our spines and our truth.

Take a Moment to Choose This Moment

Contemplate your sense of autonomy. What were you trained to do when stuck, unsure, or challenged? Did you avoid challenges? Give up quickly? Or jump in too fast before you were settled and knew what was going on? Autonomy is your ability to joyfully explore your potential, especially when you don't know what's next. That capacity lives in your observing awareness.

Autonomy Awareness Generator

Read each statement and reflect inwardly.

One way powerlessness fear causes me to relinquish autonomy is ____
____.
(e.g., it talks me out of facing my fears; it causes me to jump right into

what's going on externally before I'm clear what's going on within my-self; it requires me to obsess about what I want to face until I get over-whelmed and don't want to face it anymore)

A powerlessness belief I have about autonomy is ___________________ ____.

(e.g., I can't face this from my Essence; I could fail; I'm going to be made wrong; I don't have what it takes inside of me to face this; I feel out of control, because I can't get control of the unknown; I have to do this because it's expected or I'll be seen as weak if I don't)

One way this belief has impacted my life is ___________________ ____.

(e.g., I've said I wanted to do something and then not followed through; I lose my ability to enjoy the unknowns; it's robbed me of the antici-pation of being surprised about how I will get what I want; I've given up on myself; I've made unknowns wrong, so I resisted against them; I haven't trusted and believed in myself or my internal resources; I've harmed my connection with others by jumping in too hot, making as-sumptions without really tuning in)

One way I can face my powerlessness fear about autonomy is by _____ ____.

(e.g., validating my fear and noticing my body's response instead of catastrophizing about it; appreciating my Pleasers, Protectors, and Punishers for trying to keep me safe by avoiding unknowns and con-flict; exploring to discover the powerlessness belief)

One way I can transform this powerlessness belief is by ___________ ____.

(e.g., validating the belief as seeming like the truth because that's the treatment we received; bringing some Essencey energy to meet the body sensations of powerlessness; exploring what the need is that didn't get met, which caused the powerlessness in the first place, then meet the powerlessness need with the internal Essencey attention it never received)

One way I can trust my autonomy to enjoy unknowns and stuckness is by ______________________________________. (e.g., remembering that I have the ability to transform internal and external experiences into Essence; remembering that I have the ability to transform internal and external experiences into Essence; remembering that I have the ability to transform internal and external experiences into Essence [Giggle])

Validating Your Trained-In Experience: Autonomy

Validation: "Yes, we were trained to believe incompetence meant our sense of self was lacking."

Notice how your body responds. Do you feel openness? Tightness? Both?

Speak this *Simple Truth*: "When we're feeling like we don't know something we should, we can remind ourselves that incompetence is the first stage of learning." Notice how your body responds to empowering incompetence.

Reframe incompetence as a sign of learning, not the sense of self as lacking something. Speak this *Simple Truth*: "Thank you, uncomfortable sensations, for letting us know we're on the edge of learning." Notice the shift. What if *uncomfortable* didn't mean "bad"? Let that possibility settle into your body.

Validating Truth: "The truth about us is our uncomfortable incompetence is a signal of learning, not a character flaw of not enough."

Notice where energy flows or constricts in your body. Wrap any flowing energy you feel internally around the constricted parts with compassion. Speak another *Simple Truth*: "Thank you for showing us where we're stuck. Now we know where to bring Essence."

Speak this Validation aloud: "Yes, we were trained to believe our abilities are fixed—either we have them or we don't."

Notice your body's response. Openings? Tightenings? Marshmallow-mind integration? Invoke curiosity about the either/ors you marinated in. Listen to your inner body for memories of them to surface.

Speak this *Simple Truth*: "We believed putting in effort meant we lacked ability. But effort is what builds ability." Let this integrate by noticing your body's response.

Speak this Validating Truth aloud: "The truth about us is our intelligence, like our Essence, grows when we step off the who's-right-who's-wrong field and let ourselves explore from the truth of our worthiness instead."

Notice how your body responds. You're locating yourself in the present by noticing what's happening in the present. You're also bringing all the past versions of you into alignment with the truth about you. No more worrying about doing wrong; we're doing truth now. Not an arrogant truth—that's what defensive strategies think we need. We're talking an authentic truth that's empowered to explore on its own path.

Take a Moment to Choose This Moment

What connection pools did you swim in growing up? Were you taught to fear that the connection you needed would be too little or too much? Did you watch people stay in the shallow end of the pool to stay in connection, or did you watch people drown in the deep end of an overpowering connection? Notice what happens to your connection with your own insides as you contemplate these ponderings. Throw a life preserver to your insides by validating your worthiness of the need for connection and your courage and willingness to explore what went unmet.

Connection Awareness Generator

In our early years, being in connection with our caretakers' defensive strategies often meant that we had to limit our thriving or try to overachieve as pseudo-thriving.

I'm realizing I perceive something or someone as keeping me from thriving when ____.
(e.g., people don't acknowledge my experience; someone tells me no; someone disrespects me; my first attempt fails)

How my Heroing Pleaser reacts when I perceive that something or someone is keeping me from thriving is by ________________________.
(e.g., over-efforting to get them to see me as good; withdrawing from the connection until they are in a better mood; trying really hard to

get them to see what they are doing right in the moment, although they are physiologically incapable of seeing what they're doing [they are stuck in the distorting mind of defensive strategies]; convincing me their needs matter more than mine)

How my Villainous Punisher reacts when I perceive that something or someone is keeping me from thriving is by ________________________.
(e.g., immediately focusing only on the ways they're wrong; berating me for believing I could do it, for wanting to thrive; convincing me to withdraw my goodness from the connection because they don't deserve it; attacking them for attacking me [*They started it!*]; telling me I had to act this way because of them [justification])

Since my Heroic Pleaser and Villain-y Punisher disconnect me from my Essence, one way I could increase my capacity to connect with my Essence when I perceive I'm not thriving is by ____________________.
(e.g., giving value to my current internal experience as the gateway to uncovering the powerlessness belief and unmet need that are stuck [I know I will learn from my insides when I give my insides value]; appreciating my Pleaser and Punisher—they open up and become flexible when I bring Essence to the hard work they've done for me; cultivating my Essence voice in my head and speaking Simple Truths)

One way I can interest my Pleaser and my Punisher in their Essence quality roles is ____.
(e.g., I can coach them about the right-or-wrong system [in the right-or-wrong system, we fail; in the inner truth system, we learn and grow]; I can appreciate them for the hard work they've done to help us thrive while dragging around our powerlessness; I can feel compassion for my Pleaser and my Punisher and the limited resources from which they've had to choose [from our parents' defensive strategies]; I can model how we can get what we want [getting our needs met] more easily from Essence)

The way to increase your capacity for deeper connections with your inner self and others is to transform your powerlessness beliefs and defensive strategies. They are struggling to connect without connecting to the inner Essencey resources that can create authentic connection.

Validating Your Trained-In Experience: Connection

Validation: "Yes, we were trained to believe that connection sometimes feels free and sometimes limits our thriving."

Notice your connection to your own inner body. You might feel the openness of the truth and the tightness of believing you had to be a certain way to stay connected. As soon as you become the observing awareness noticing your body sensations, you start to feel connected to your deepest inner self.

Speak this *Simple Truth*: "I'm integrating how our powerlessness beliefs about who we get to be in connection require us to give our power away to others to try and stay connected."

Notice how your body connects to this truth. Does your inner body relax? Do you take an easy breath in? Do you feel some fear as tightness or constriction in your belly?

Simple Truth: "We give our power away and then try to take it back with our defensive strategies."

Notice how your body responds to this awareness of the wasted, misaligned energies competing inside for what is true about you in connection to others.

Your connection to your own inner self is so important and valuable it deserves another *Simple Truth*: "I'm realizing connection brings up all our sense-of-self threats about who we really are and whether we get to thrive while staying connected to those we love."

Notice how your body responds to the possibility of being able to thrive in connection. We can't be thriving and giving our power away at the same time.

Validating Truth: "The truth about our worthiness in connection is we are worthy of thriving while connecting."

Notice how your body responds. Open for business in there? Or closing off into some leftover fear?

Connecting *Simple Truth*: "I'm putting together how we can only have the body-felt experience of thriving in our worthiness when we are connected to our Essence resources through our body/mind connection."

Notice how your body responds. Any effervescence popping? Cool. Some fearful tightening erupting? Cool. You never know what needs your Essencey attention inside to transform until you go inside and check. Validate what emerges.

Embedded within our Essence qualities, we feel deeply connected to ourselves and deeply connected to life. Consumed by powerlessness beliefs and defensive strategies, we feel disconnected and alienated from everything good, activating a desperation to get the good back. Whichever of these physiological states we are in has a profound impact on what we perceive is happening to us. When we're connected to our Essence qualities, we don't experience the threat of anything being done "to us" to keep us from thriving. We feel open to connect with others and available to help each other thrive.

In powerlessness and defensive strategies, though, the perception of a threat to keep us from thriving is a constant unwanted companion, shutting down our openness to authentic connection. Resisting a threat keeps us from thriving by keeping us out of our Essence qualities. We give our power away but blame others for taking it. Many of us learned that being in connection with another meant we would be kept from thriving.

EPILOGUE

"The moment you change your perception from
closed and guarded to open and Essencey is the
moment you rewrite the chemistry of your body. A
new perception and new body chemistry transform
your identity from powerlessness to powerful, allowing you to have new experiences of being satisfied
and fulfilled authentically."

—Joni L. Davis

The Beginning of Loss

In late 2019, I began losing the hair on the top of my head. It started
with a bald spot on my left side the size of three quarters side by side.
Yeah, that's a big strip of baldness. I changed my part to the right, only
to lose hair there too. Headbands became my daily accessory. Grief
and disorientation overtook me. I knew this wasn't fatal, but I was
drowning in an identity crisis. I wasn't just losing hair; I was losing
who I thought I was.

I spiraled into fear. I couldn't sleep, I couldn't think straight, and
my body was constantly on alert. The question that haunted me: *What*

did I do wrong? Even though I knew that was a Victim Powerlessness Perception. I started seeing doctors, enduring sterile exam rooms filled with other women who, like me, felt helpless. The fear in the room was tangible. Compassion was scarce. I felt invisible. Desperate. I clung to the hope that someone would tell me what was happening and how to fix it.

Eventually, I received a diagnosis: lichen planopilaris, an autoimmune disease in which my immune system was attacking my hair. Relief at having an answer quickly gave way to devastation. The doctors said the damage was permanent. I tried everything—steroid creams, stem cell injections, and even Plaquenil, which can cause macular degeneration. Every treatment seemed to make things worse. I was living in fear. My every decision was soaked in powerlessness.

A glimpse of power

I cried. A lot. I was drowning in the question, *What did I do to deserve this?* Even with all my study of powerlessness beliefs, I was stuck. Then, during a podcast with Gay Hendricks, something clicked: He spoke about putting your body in the perfect physiological state for conscious luck to happen. I realized my fear-based physiology was sabotaging my healing.

I remembered Dan Siegel's Wheel of Awareness and my Bicycle Wheel of Awareness. Remembering to locate my sense of self in the hub and watching the activity out on the rim gave me the distance and space from my current scary experience to be able to settle my powerlessness flare-ups. From the hub I could think creatively instead of reactively.

I made a commitment: to transform my powerlessness and reclaim my body's healing potential. I began talking to my fears instead of believing them. I validated them, acknowledged them, and soothed them. With my body and mind finally at ease, I could think clearly again. Curiosity returned.

I noticed how I was giving away my power and validated my fears and unmet needs until I could feel my internal experience of power returning. I was more balanced and settled inside so I could notice a pattern: flare-ups every six months. I asked myself, *What am I putting in my body twice a year that mimics hair?* The answer: collagen. And then it hit me—I had been getting facial filler injections biannually.

Healing with Essence

I stopped the fillers and started practicing visual imagery with validating meditations. If fear could influence my body, so could Essence. Slowly, my hair began to grow back. Not all of it, but enough. I no longer needed headbands. I had a real part again, at least on my right side. I was learning to love my bald spot as a symbol of my courage to learn instead of suffering. And very importantly, I had taken my power back.

I discovered that when I communicated with my body from Essence, it responded. I pictured joyful, dancing hair follicles and imagined my mother's face telling me, *It's safe to fully thrive.* Although my mother never said this in real life, I knew she would have if she had known how. Her happy face, even if just from one memory, became the soothing image I paired with Simple Truths in my meditations.

The cosmic joke

Then came the lump in my breast. I found it myself, and soon after, I was diagnosed with breast cancer. The irony? I had fought so hard to save my hair only to lose it all to chemo.

But I had learned how to transform fear. I used the same imagery and Essencey Validations I had used for my hair to support my body through chemo. I invited my cancer cells to return to Essence. I didn't make my cancer cells wrong. I knew my extreme powerlessness hair fears had confused them about how to thrive. I gave my body messages of cooperation and healing.

My tumor, initially the size of a Double Stuf Oreo, responded. It shrank significantly. When I asked my doctor to feel it, he was shocked.

He had assumed it started small because now he couldn't feel it at all. This allowed me to receive a lumpectomy instead of a mastectomy.

Trusting myself among experts

After three rounds of a six-round protocol of chemo, my body said, *Enough*. I was having severe allergic reactions to the chemo, fevers of 103°, chills, and intense whole-body rashes. But the protocol called for three more rounds. My doctor wanted to stick to the protocol because nothing less had worked in the clinical trials. I was torn between trusting my intuition and following expert advice. My doctor said let's do one more round, and we'll up the Benadryl to handle the allergic response, I did one more round of chemo and had my worst reaction yet. Finally, my doctor agreed to stop. I believe it was because I had trusted my intuitions and asked him to feel the tumor before.

After surgery, the cancer was 99 percent gone. The surgeon said that was "unheard of."

I knew it wasn't unheard of. It was Essence. It was presence. It was the physiological state of healing that I had learned to create within myself. I also learned to listen to my body. My body didn't want things in it that weren't it.

Since I've had both experiences of facing medical trauma from Essence (breast cancer) and from fear (autoimmune disorder/extreme hair loss), I've learned that a body in Essence heals faster and needs less medicine than a body in fear. My experience has taught me that an Essence-filled body is sensitive and responsive to the truth within it, whereas a fear-filled body is confused about what is true about its optimal functioning. Wow—powerlessness fear confuses our sense of self and our body about what is true about our optimal functioning.

Where to go from here

You have traveled far. You've discovered how to meet seventeen unmet emotional needs. (That's a lot!) You've also explored and practiced how to turn toward your inner experiences with compassion. You've tried on the experience of validating yourself in ways your caregivers couldn't. This is what it means to love yourself.

You've learned that fear-based body/mind states trap us in victimhood and confuse the body about how it should function. And Essence-based states open the door to power, healing, and connection. You're deepening your knowing that your inner experiences matter, that your body is listening. You're expanding your awareness and trust that your Essence is always available.

When your nervous system is settled, your perception is clear. When you validate your experience, you respond with presence. You don't have to be perfect to be worthy. You were always worthy. You just needed someone to validate your Essence. Now you can be that someone for yourself.

Whatever your political party, be in that party FROM Essence every moment, instead of justifying current behavior or getting seduced into judgments about other people.

Whatever your religious beliefs, function FROM your Essence each moment within those beliefs so you can trust that you're living from your beliefs and not stepping outside of them when you automatically get defensive.

Whatever your life challenges, face them FROM Essence moment to moment, not just when it's easy.

Whatever bad things someone thinks about you while they're in their defensive strategies, face it FROM your Essence moment to moment instead of suffering or retaliating.

Each moment, live, express, choose, love, explore, repair, thrive, and create FROM your Essence by transforming the powerlessness and defensive parts of you that never were your Essence.

Take a Moment to Choose This Moment

Look at the Essence qualities list and pick one that you'd
like to integrate more into your moment-to-moment
experience. For example, maybe you want to explore
how to feel more empowered. Power is an Essence
quality that allows you to feel your impact on your own
experience and experiences all around you. It is your
ability to see yourself as a creator instead of a reactor.

To activate this empowered part of you, you need to understand
the players inside that see through the lens of disempowerment: your
Pleasers, Protectors, Punishers, and powerlessness. Notice how your
Pleasers, Protectors, and Punishers try to feel empowered. Notice how
you've been trained to feel powerless about activating certain authentic
aspects of yourself. For example, notice how your Pleasers, Protectors,
Punishers, and powerlessness talk to you in your head and convince
you of your yeses and noes. Their yeses and noes will be based in fear
and give your power away, like trying not to upset someone else or
trying not to be the one who's doing it wrong. Then contemplate your
authentic yeses and noes. Your authentic yeses and noes ground you in
your power. Where do you feel these in your body? What does your
authentic voice sound like inside? How could you learn how to discern
the difference between these voices? Validate the aspects of you that
you want to transform, so they can begin to trust that there is a new
power in town.

We've all grown up in a culture that's trying to produce good
human beings, and deep down in the very core of our being, we all
know that we are good human beings. We just haven't known about
the side of us that isn't connected to our Essence qualities, and so we

don't know how to trust accessing them internally. We've been grasping for external resources that activate this internal Essencey part of us. We've seen what that does to us. Now—more than ever—is the time to tap into our internal Essence resources so we are the change we want to see in the world.

We all want something to believe in so much that we can envision the future where we feel good about being with each other. A place where we can trust each other as inherently good and functioning from internal goodness. Now that you know that the only thing that convinces us to behave in ways outside of our internal goodness, our Essence qualities, is powerlessness fear, you understand that you have a big choice to make each moment: Face what's happening from Essence or from powerless fear, defensively Stacked.

The more we remind each other that we are truly our Essence and not our fear-Stacked selves, the more we believe that humans are good and worthy of stewarding these bodies, each other, other species, and the planet. Let's start with your belief. Validate Essence to believe.

My belief is big. But it wasn't always. Knowing the skills within this book, especially Validation, is what allows me to feel the truth inside of me so deeply that my fears are no longer a match for it. My belief in your Essence is big. May this book strengthen your belief, making it so big that you no longer get tangled in the who's-right-who's-wrong power struggles that destroy belief in Essence while allegedly fighting for it.

Validate Essence to spread belief.

Let your explorations continue from here. Validate to regulate. Let your Essence lead.

You are worthy of fully thriving.

Remember, take internal actions first to change your external actions.

Internal Actions to Transform Powerlessness into Essence Power

♡ Self-reflect about the 17 powerlessness beliefs that imprint from the 17 unmet needs.

♡ Validate the powerlessness belief as the training you received and not the truth about you.

♡ Get your mind interested in how your body is responding as the way to give value to your internal experience.

♡ Notice how your emotional and nervous systems settle when you give value to your internal experience.

♡ Notice how your attentional and sense-of-self systems settle when you give value to your internal experience.

♡ Speak a Validating Truth to your insides directly relating to the powerlessness belief.

♡ Focus your mind on how your body responds to this Validating Truth.

♡ Notice when you turn your attention inward, your mind and body work together, opening a deeper connection to your Essence and to life around you.

♡ Create the experience you want to have from your infinite Essence resources.

♡ Moment by moment, notice if you're seeing things through Powerlessness, Protector, Punisher, Pleaser, or Essence.

ACKNOWLEDGMENTS

I'm so grateful to Kathy for pullin' it all together for us over and over in all ways that make you a very special being. To Maurie for listening to me consciously and unconsciously complain about what I can and can't do until I come to my senses. And the biggest, warmest hug of thankfulness to everyone who walked with me on this journey— family, friends, teachers, and mentors. A big "shout out about Essence" to Katie Hendricks and Julie Colwell, and especially the brave souls who trusted me to walk with them on their own journeys of transformation, my lovable and so very worthy clients. To Gay Hendricks, who taught me how to fill my body with the energy of Essence no matter what environment I'm in.

APPENDIX

ValidNation

When I was in school to become a therapist, we were learning about group therapy's basic premise that the group can only grow as much as its most stuck member. We're learning here that stuckness means that the person has been trained to not trust their authenticity, their Essence. Double-check and see if your stuckness is holding you back and therefore unconsciously holding others back by wondering, *How do my Pleasers, Protectors, and Punishers help me get my needs met, but end up keeping me from being my authentic self?*

For example, your Pleaser might desperately need to feel so good about the self that it can't look at the ways that it doesn't feel good. Your Protector might keep you complaining about all the reasons why you can't do the thing you say you want to do, so you don't have to face your fear of not being good enough. Your Punisher might convince you that you have to withdraw your love and caring from someone until they love you the right way. They are all stuck in crazy strategies when they are seen out in the light, huh? Wonder about how your Essence could handle each of these situations and then step into your Essence and go. Validate to be authentic.

Take a Moment to Choose This Moment

Be curious about the difference between having the
information and having the experience. Our Essence
is already having the wanted inner truth experience,
so it needs less outside information to sense and know
the truth.

Pleasers, Protectors, and Punishers move information and facts around. They organize information into right or wrong categories, so they can do things right, because they don't know how to have the experience of inner rightness, inner experiential truth. They don't know how to have the Essence experience so they're using information to try to get there. It looks like we are now an information society because our Pleasers, Protectors, and Punishers need more and more information to be righter and righter.

Make a commitment to yourself to first notice how you use and gather information to try to have a certain Essencey experience inside. Then validate the young versions of you inside that were trying to make sense of the world when no one was making sense of it for you: "Yes, we were trained to believe that the world is big and confusing and out of control, and we're not going be taught how to make sense of it." Notice how your body responds to connecting with a part of you that is so young and shows up as body sensations. In this moment, be to this young version of yourself what someone couldn't be for you, a guide to inner truth. *Validating Truth*: "The truth is located inside of us and not in external information gathering." Notice how your body responds. Make a note of where truth lives in your body. Memorize the path. Contemplate making this path, your moment-to-moment path.

I would like to propose that to be a ValidNation, a nation of validators growing validated human beings, we need to step outside of the who's-right-who's-wrong system and back into the truth.

Both are ways we're trying to get to the truth. The who's-right-who's-wrong version, unfortunately, puts our autonomic nervous system on alert. This dysregulates us into our fears of being the wrong one or doing it wrong and requires the armor of our defenses. We're all noticing how we treat each other when our sense of self has been trained to be fused with our fears of wrongness (unworthiness) and our defensive strategies.

I invite you to challenge yourself and those that you touch with your Essence, to learn to speak, think, and act from Simple Truth.

You can accomplish the same thing that you're trying to accomplish with the who's-right-who's-wrong system, namely, trying to be a good person taking part in a benevolent world, by learning to think and act and express in a way that doesn't make anyone or anything right or wrong. You simply know the truth, that if you want to connect with another, Essence to Essence, both of your autonomic nervous systems need to be relaxed and regulated, safe from the evaluation of right-or-wrong threat.

So, you speak Simple Truth when everyone's regulated to maintain the relaxed environment. And, when activation of the fear and defensive structure happens, which it will, you validate the need, the experience, or the feeling until everyone in your environment, including yourself, is back to safe and sound in the truth.

This is the way—shout-out to *The Mandalorian*—you get to experience the freedom and empowerment of creating what you want, instead of suffering from what you don't want.

Lastly, to motivate ourselves to create such a big change in our lives, we need to give more value to the change we want to make than to the current stuck pattern. How do we do this? Catch the meanings that your Pleasers, Protectors, and Punishers give to the change. Have compassion for how they've been trained to keep your identity the same even though it may not be in Essence. Validate the value that the current stuck pattern has had for you up until now.

Validation: "Yes, we were trained to believe the way to be a good human being is by stepping out of our Essence and stepping into people-pleasing, protecting, and punishing to belong and not be all alone."

Notice how that brilliant and vibrant inner body of yours responds. You might feel sad, afraid, or mad. You might notice openness or tightness. Observe it all from a compassionate (nonevaluative) place. Notice what happens to your inner states when you observe them nonjudgmentally.

Simple Truth: "I feel you, little Essences. I know we're scared to fully emerge as the powerful creative being that we are."

Notice how your Essencey little kiddos inside respond to being seen for what they have always been.

Validating Truth: "The truth about us is our Essence is who we truly are, and we can trust this by feeling the truth as openness, expansion, and empowerment in our body."

Once the stuck, non-Essencey pattern is validated as trying to help us in some significant way, this part of us opens and relaxes so that it can learn and grow in new ways. Once your Pleasers, Protectors, Punishers, and powerlessness experience Essence, they open to creative ways to get needs met instead of reactive ways.

Together, we can transform. From the inside out. Let's go for it!

GLOSSARY

Autonomic nervous system: Located in our brain stem, not our cortex, this system runs under our awareness until we generate awareness of it. It is our sense-of-self threat alert mode.

Defensive mode/Defensive strategies: How a person reacts when the body contracts and the mind constricts into a narrow perception, believing that the self must arm itself to survive.

Essence mode: The state when the body is relaxed and the mind is open, so the person can feel their access to their internal resources, their Essence qualities.

Essencey: A word I made up to describe things that are connected to our inner Essence resources.

Internal body: Your inner state of felt experience—more specifically, what the energy in your body is doing. Is it flowing or constricting?

Observing awareness: The sense of yourself back behind your body sensations, feelings, thoughts, and actions. The caring witness who's watching your internal experience in real time.

Parasympathetic nervous system: A branch of the autonomic nervous system that defensively shuts us down during perceived threat or comforts and soothes our fears when in Essence.

Powerlessness beliefs: Thoughts that erupt from body sensations, as if they signal something is wrong with the sense of self.

Powerlessness sensations: Body sensations we've been trained to label as "us" that are actually memories of past pain.

Sense of self: The body-felt experience of being you—how you identify as fear or Essence.

Simple Truth: A statement that is truthful about experiences in a way that doesn't make anyone or anything right or wrong. They emerge from deep channels of Essence within.

Stacked: The physiological state of experiencing powerlessness in the body, where the sense of self leaves the body to reside in the head, running nonauthentic defensive strategies.

Sympathetic nervous system: A branch of the autonomic nervous system that revs us up into excitement (Essence) or fear depending on how it was trained before we could talk.

Validating Truths: Statements that give value to the truth that has always lived inside of each of us. They start with the lead line "The truth about us is . . ."

Validations: Statements that give value to experiences without making anyone or anything right or wrong. Validations give value as the way to cultivate change. They often start with the lead line "Yes, we were trained to believe . . ."

Victim powerlessness perception: The narrow and collapsed perception that we all see ourselves and the world through when our powerlessness is auto-activated. This is the lens of the part of us that wasn't validated and therefore doesn't know how to feel empowered or see through an empowering lens.

We/Us: Including your present-moment sense of self and all the past versions of you who show up as body sensations of unmet needs.

Who's-right-who's-wrong system: A system of what makes a good person imposed from external sources because the individual was not taught to access their inner truth.

REFERENCES

Colwell, Julie. 2014. *The Relationship Skills Workbook*. St Martin's Essentials.

Colwell, Julie. 2019. *The Relationship Ride*. Integrity Arts Press.

Colwell, Julie. 2020. *The Inner Map*. Integrity Arts Press.

Damasio, Antonio. 2010. *Self Comes to Mind*. Vintage.

Fitzgerald, F. Scott. 1934. *Tender Is the Night*. Charles Scribner's Sons.

Hendricks, Gay. 1982. *Learning to Love Yourself*. Prentice-Hall.

Hendricks, Gay. 2009. *The Big Leap*. HarperCollins.

Hendricks, Gay. 2022. *Conscious Luck*. St. Martin's Essentials.

Hendricks, Katie, and Gay Hendricks. 1991. *Radiance!* Bookpeople.

Hendricks, Katie, and Gay Hendricks. 1992. *Conscious Loving*. Bantam Books.

Hendricks, Katie, and Gay Hendricks. 1999. *The Conscious Heart*. Bantam Books.

Hendricks, Katie, and Gay Hendricks. 2014. *Hearts in Harmony*. E-book, Amare Inc.

Hendricks, Katie, and Gay Hendricks. 2017. *At the Speed of Life*. CreateSpace Independent Publishing Platform.

Lao Tzu. *Tao Te Ching*. Penguin Random House.

Porges, Stephen. 1994. *The Polyvagal Theory*. Norton & Company.

Schore, Allan. 1994. *Affect Regulation and the Origin of the Self*. Routledge.

Schore, Allan. 2003. *Affect Dysregulation and Disorders of the Self*. W.W. Norton & Company.

Schore, Allan. 2003. *Affect Regulation and the Repair of the Self.* Routledge.

Schore, Allan. 2012. *The Science of the Art of Psychotherapy.* W.W. Norton & Company.

Schore, Allan. 2021. *The Right Brain and the Origin of Human Nature.* W.W. Norton & Company.

Siegel, Dan. 2010. *Mindsight.* Random House Publishing Group.

Siegel, Dan. 2012. *The Developing Mind.* The Guilford Press.

Siegel, Dan. 2018. *Aware.* TarcherPerigee.

Siegel, Dan. 2022. *Intraconnected.* W.W. Norton & Company.

Siegel, Dan. 2022. *Personality and Wholeness in Therapy.* W.W. Norton & Company.

Walker, Alice. 2000. *The Way Forward Is with a Broken Heart.* Random House Books.

ABOUT THE AUTHOR

JONI L. DAVIS has been interested in the ways people change (and do not change) for over thirty years. She is a licensed marriage and family therapist (MS, LMFT) specializing in childhood/developmental trauma, complex PTSD, relationships, and body-centered awareness. She lives in Long Beach, California, where she connects with nature every day on her bike rides into the office with her two little dogs in the basket. Transform is her first book, inspired by her own journey and over two decades of practicing therapy.